'dialectic'
 civ. — 1–17, 49–50, 52
          93–4 97 105

'method' — 40, 62, 102

Rethinking Historicism

Rethinking Historicism
Critical Readings in Romantic History

Marjorie Levinson, Marilyn Butler,
Jerome McGann, Paul Hamilton

Basil Blackwell

Copyright © Marjorie Levinson, Marilyn Butler, Jerome McGann, Paul Hamilton 1989

First published 1989

Basil Blackwell Ltd
108 Cowley Road, Oxford, OX4 1JF, UK

Basil Blackwell Inc.
432 Park Avenue South, Suite 1503
New York, NY 10016, USA

All rights reserved. Except for the quotation of short passages for the purposes of criticism and review, no part of this publication may be reproduced, stored in a retrieval system, or transmitted, in any form or by any means, electronic, mechanical, photocopying, recording or otherwise, without the prior permission of the publisher.

Except in the United States of America, this book is sold subject to the condition that it shall not, by way of trade or otherwise, be lent, re-sold, hired out, or otherwise circulated without the publisher's prior consent in any form of binding or cover other than that in which it is published and without a similar condition including this condition being imposed on the subsequent purchaser.

British Library Cataloguing in Publication Data

Rethinking historicism: critical readings in Romantic history.
1. English literature, 1745–1837. Romanticism—Critical studies
I. Levinson, Marjorie, 1957–
820.9′145

ISBN 0–631–16591–6

Library of Congress Cataloging in Publication Data

Rethinking historicism: critical readings in romantic history /
Marjorie Levinson . . . [et al.].
 p. cm.
Includes index.
ISBN 0–631–16591–6
1. Historicism. 2. Romanticism. 3. Criticism. I. Levinson, Marjorie.
PN98.H57R48 1989
809′.93358—dc19   88–31866
                                                                                  CIP

Typeset in 11 on 13pt Baskerville
Printed in Great Britain at
The Camelot Press Ltd, Southampton

Contents

	Introduction *Marjorie Levinson*	1
1	The New Historicism: Back to the Future *Marjorie Levinson*	18
2	Repossessing the Past: the Case for an Open Literary History *Marilyn Butler*	64
3	The Third World of Criticism *Jerome McGann*	85
4	Keats and Critique *Paul Hamilton*	108
	Index	143

Introduction

Marjorie Levinson

'"Chaque époque rêve la suivante." (*Michelet. Avenir! Avenir!*)'
To which Benjamin adds, by way of consummation, the all-important afterthought: 'Not merely does each age dream the next one, but it aims, in so doing, to awaken.'
Irving Wohlfarth, 'The Historian as Chiffonier'

... works of art, and that includes the so-called individualistic ones, speak the language of a 'We', not of an 'I', and they do so to the extent to which they refrain from conforming in some extrinsic fashion to that 'We' and its idiom.
Theodor Adorno, Aesthetic Theory

We have had more than enough reflections on 'the new historicism'. As Edward Pechter observed last year, 'simply to write about *the* new historicism is to construct a fiction, a critical fabrication, like the Elizabethan World Picture or the Medieval Mind.'[1] Still, as Pechter's own proceedings show, one can, with perfect logic, recognize 'the many different and even contradictory critical practices [which] are currently represented as new historicism' and at the same time search out the political recesses, past and present, of this strangely monologic projection.[2] The four essays in this collection maintain just such a double awareness. All of us, wary of making a fetish of this new look, hope to illuminate by our reading practice the reality of its appearance. Our essays will be found to reflect in some metacritical way – procedural, rhetorical, philosophical – the phenomenon around and within which this project took shape. Rather than isolate the leading points of these four essays which emerged so variously and which differ so widely in their method, study texts and tone, I'd like to describe that second-order address.

Of the four pieces presented here, two were delivered at a

conference in honour of Carl Woodring, entitled 'Romanticism, Politics, and the New Historicism', UCLA, 1985. My own essay was written for that occasion, while Jerry McGann's was intended for inclusion in his *Social Values and Poetic Acts*, 1988. The other two studies are the work of British scholars sympathetic to the positions taken by the American essays. Marilyn Butler delivered a shorter version of her contribution to this volume for her inaugural address as Regius Professor, Cambridge, 1987.[3]

All four essays depict the possibilities of a historicist project when it is conceived and conducted as a reflexive affair and when reflection, an act of mind, is set in the field of material production, its cultural mediations and their hegemonic forms. Each elaborates the idea that a reading of the past which is not also and integrally a reflected operation on the present betrays its received historicist premises: namely, to reveal the past, the object, either as it is/was in itself, or as it is intended in the sympathetic consciousness of the present. Further, as those dated phrases might suggest, we hope that our drive towards dialectical closure will produce a new set of terms for our encounters with the past. The idea is to sidestep historicism's Hobson's choice of contemplation or empathy: in the Romantic idiom, knowledge or power. If there is one single insight peculiar to the postmodern condition, it might be the realization that both those attitudes, however different the methods they endorse, are in the service of a rigged dialectic: a subjectively privileged and also armoured affair. Moreover, by rewriting 'knowledge' as possession *of* the object, and 'power' as possession *by* the object, we begin to appreciate both high ambitions as reflections of the commodity form. Like that form, both possessions negate another and primary concept: production. Both, then, traitors to the very humanism they serve, must be counted idealisms of a peculiarly motivated – materially interested – kind.

We would be foolish to claim originality for the notion that any genuine criticism of an object is, in the very instance of that exercise, a reflexive critique. As we all know, this Hegelian inflection of a Kantian theme shapes such keynote Romantic works as *The Prelude*, 'The Cenci' and 'The Fall of Hyperion', not to mention a host of more retiring but no less epochal poems. It might even be described as *the* ethico-epistemological feature subtending our formal use of the category-term, Romantic.

Introduction

The readings developed in this book depart from that model in their working concept of reference and causality, one which collapses subject and object positions (and with them, signifier and signified, mind and matter, cause and effect) into different determinations of a single action. I take Shelley's familiar analysis from the Preface to *Prometheus Unbound* for my contrastive instance. 'Poets . . . are, in one sense, the creators, and, in another, the creations, of their age.' (And, I remind the reader that Marilyn Butler sets this quotation as the headnote to her paradigm-breaking book, *Romantics, Rebels and Reactionaries*, 1982.) The balanced periods of Shelley's sentence, with their crisp bracketing of active from passive moments and agencies, obscure just what these essays reveal. As Shelley's own authorial practice consistently demonstrates, the poets create *themselves* as creatures – 'creations' – of the age and they do so by *refusing* what is given to them as the age. Their manner of negating the given – in Coleridge's language, when 'a subject . . . becomes a subject by the act of constructing itself objectively to itself', and, in today's parlance, 'contestation' – is the determined expression of an epochal spirit which, paradoxically, comes into being with and *only* with that repetition.[4]

To illustrate this paradox, I offer a short, schematic account of Marilyn Butler's contribution to this volume. In the first and most arresting phase of her argument, Butler brings to our notice the popular, progressive and above all Enlightened gestures of Southey's quest romance, *Thalaba the Destroyer*, a poem excluded from our canons both by its supposed mediocrity and by the politics of its form – a politics assumed to be those of the servile laureate and thus, decidedly unRomantic. In a second phase, Butler adds Southey's freshly registered voice to that intertextual conversation poem we call 'the Romantic age'. Within that changed environment, a number of poems that, by their lights as well as our own, take a formally and doctrinally advanced line, betray their deeply chartered and, in effect, pre-emptive heterodoxy. We learn how such 'majority' poets as Wordsworth, Coleridge, and even Byron, by their critical *resistance* to Southey's sensational and, in that politicized field, *sectarian* imagination, produced themselves as a force for reaction, then and now, far more potent than Southey, for all his standard bearing.

Butler's reassessment is no mere inversion or inflation, actions proceeding from subject to object, present to past, difference to identity. The new view emerges through an epochal interdetermination, an exercise at once described in the essay (an Enlightenment/Romantic affair) and, in the modern instance of Butler's own Romancing, enacted by it. These two actions are not independent; neither is it a question of new aspects coming to light (nor, of course, of 'subjective' truths). Butler doesn't show us a fact that was there all along, waiting to be found. What we have is rather one historical fact (the conservative, defensive and self-mystifying politics of that *genuinely* critical experiment, the interior quest romance) *produced* by another. That 'other' fact is the political *offence* executed by Butler's cool descriptive method when that circumspect rationality is set beside the repressive, dehumanizing and absolutist rationalism which is Thatcher's libidinal address to the nation.[5] (Butler's ongoing interest in major–minor questions, an interest she openly politicizes in her introductory remarks, is of course part of this determined offence.) The absence of theory from Butler's work is, I believe (I speak of reasons and meanings, not purposes and causes), an act of sabotage. Thus does Butler undermine the deeply abstract objectivity used to legitimate the deeply concrete interests of the groups in power. My phrase, 'abstract objectivity', is a name for the government's rule-by-*efficiency*, a concept underwritten by 'reason and common sense' (in other words, principle and precedent: both, ideal forms) and abstracted from concrete conditions: that is, efficiency for whom, by what means, with what 'side'-effects, and towards what social/global end. Butler is not the only British critic to wield this loaded methodological discretion. One thinks, for example, of John Barrell's work. His faultlessly historicized and, so it seems, non-propositional deployment of the major Marxist themes and categories, carries a similar subversive charge. To point up the underlying logic of both methods, their *complementary* assaults on the empowered position, I quote the following reflection on dialectic.

> Genuine refutation must penetrate the power of the opponent and meet him on the ground of his strength; the case is not won by attacking him somewhere else and defeating him where he is not.[6]

This quotation from Hegel (in terms of *Butler's* values and method, a most unnatural voice), explains the strong dialectical opposition at work within Butler's elegant qualifications of the canon, and also, it tells us that there is more than rhetorical strategy at stake in that method. Dialectic is, above all, *immanent* critique; it allows no distinction of matter and method. If it persuades, it also brings a truth into being. The exemplary English modesty of Butler's scholarly style is, then, not only a deeply political and critical fact, it is a peculiarly productive fact. *Only* a method so charged – so specifically situated – could produce the historical fact: viz., the 'good' and also 'Romantic' politics of Southey's 'trash', the 'bad' and, in a changed sense, 'Romantic' politics of Wordsworth's, Coleridge's and Byron's treasures. At the same time, it is something, or some *things*, about that historical fact that will one day be found – be *made*, that is – to explain the method that produced it. Both projects, the critic's and the poets', yield up a vision of ideology, its truths and treasons (the truths *of* its treasons), that has nothing to do with the reflective/expressive/homologous affair that dominates our new historicisms, and, that loses nothing in concrete explanatory value either. Indeed, Butler's non-theorized but also antipositivist elaboration of ideology (no one makes us see so clearly as she the difference between a 'referent' and a 'signified') works a tremendous change at the level of category knowledge. Simply to read her map is to see in the canonization of those Romantic rebels not just our own idealizing interests – that is to say, ourselves as a Romantic cause – but also, the *effect* of the poets' disguised retrenchments: our myth-making a return upon their own angelic restraint.

There is a second paradox. From the standpoint of a future that gives a local habitation and name to that truth which, in its first phase, goes imageless, this possessed negation is also the poets' *break* with the age. Our critical practice – the way we produce our lives – finds out the prophecy in the Romantic exercise. That canon can now be seen to have anticipated the very critique that marks out its error. Indeed, our own Romanticism, or what goes by the name 'new historicism' in nineteenth-century studies, emerges as the prescribed critical form of the poetry we claim to de-mystify. '[The poet's] thoughts are the germs of the flower and fruit of latest time.' Moreover, by comparison with that poetry – a discourse saturated with concrete contradictions – our historicism takes shape as an impoverished, emasculated thing. It would seem that the self-criticism executed by works of poetry amounts to a third and much-belated phase: a raising to the status of a named theme that second-nature which is given to an age through its freedom to *negate* the given in an act of self-creation. Naturally, the critically *realizing* name is also a falsification of the very theme it perfects.

This problematizing of its own ideologies – ideas and methods – is not of course built into the intentional structure of the work nor is it available to contemporary readers. It emerges in all those betrayals, indiscretions and illogic (what McGann likes to call the 'non-normative') that materialize when the peculiarly detailed and concrete ideological forms of the past enter the domain of the present, where they collide, as it were, with their own future.[7] At the same time, the present, which pursues *its* project in self-creation by an action upon a past held to be the inert, isolated object of its scrutiny, produces a set of logical flaws that identify *its* historicity as an effect of its Romantic object but also, as a vision of the next judgement. 'Veil after veil may be undrawn, and the inmost naked beauty of the meaning never exposed.' Or, following Byron's dry muse, the poets' truths are always 'all before them, or behind'.

To propose that a truly historicist project is also a presentist project actualized by way of the future is only to alter the accents which have governed our reading of the Romantic ideology. That diacritical shift compels us to see ourselves as objectively involved in that ideology in a way constitutive for *both* actions, the Romantic and Romanticist. By construing our critical acts as the effect of a Romantic cause which is immanent in that effect and *only* there – or rather, *here* – we develop something which is as much difference as it is identity.

We can begin exploring this curiosity – I'll do no more than outline the strategy – by way of Spinoza. Like Shelley, we find in Spinoza's postulate of a single, irreducible substance available under two distinct and incommensurable attributes, extension and thought, a fresh purchase on the valorized antinomies generated by the static, Kantian model and also, by Hegel's dynamic emplotment of that design. Simply, we use Spinoza to set aside the array of unsurpassable dualisms that continues to shape our critical discourse, idealizing and de-mystifying alike. Where, for example, I characterize today's address towards the past as a matter of 'cause and effect', I mean to describe the relation between today's concept of its Romantic object (a mode of substance conceived under the attribute of thought, or, subjectivity), and a literary-historical entity (that same mode conceived under the attribute of extension: or, the objective). Since the concept and the object are *one thing*, positioned within incommensurable systems, what we call 'cause' – say, the new historicism – is also the effect of its Romantic object. This, theoretically derived fact has not escaped observation by our keener commentators on this rage for history. Returning to Shelley, 'creating the age' is also the most totalized effect *of* that age, revealed in all its necessity in the practice of some particular future. This, then – this bracketing between an overdetermining past and a future perfect – is the 'subjection [from] which the loftiest do not escape'. It is Althusser (his shocking drop in academic prestige must be taken as symptomatic) who has imagined this figure in philosophic form. His name for it – for a way of thinking 'the effectivity of the whole on its parts' when 'wholeness' is conceived transhistorically – is 'structural causality'. Shelley called it Demogorgon.

Each of these essays in some way makes itself the object of its own created subject: namely, 'the text' reproduced under the aspect of 'the work'. Each puts its own reading in jeopardy of the past it has read by discovering itself as both cause and effect of that constructed past. In our essays, the bounding outline is situated as an efficient, not a final cause. By the determinacy of our arguments, we call up certain matters-of-fact which *escape* that mental form, internally and at the edges. This excess – a cultivated disorder – puts each of our critiques, each 'firm perswasion', both within and beyond the Romantic ideology, the object of its exercise.

> Our own image comes back to us from the mirror of the literary absolute [or, from the literature we absolutize through our criticism]. And the massive truth flung back at us is that *we have not left the era of the subject* . . . *[We] are all, still and always, aware of the* Crisis, *convinced that 'interventions' are necessary and that the least of texts is immediately effective*; we all think, as if it went without saying, that politics passes through the literary (or the theoretical). Romanticism is our *naïveté* [but not] our error. (my emphasis)[8]

What Philippe Lacoue-Labarthes and Jean-Luc Nancy, the

authors of the above quotation, characterize as a 'repetitive compulsion', I will describe, following Dominick LaCapra, as 'a complex repetitive temporality' realized through the psychoanalytically defined phenomenon of transference: not, in this context, a 'compulsion', but a determined operation *upon* that compelled thing – an experiment.[9] We are not, 'all' and 'always', Romantic subjects. We who are practising Romanticist criticism today *make* ourselves Romantic subjects (and also *objects* of the Romantic knowledge) in so far as we elucidate the poems of the early nineteenth century in a particular and particularly unfree fashion.

Nor are we 'still', as Jerome Christensen has recently proposed, Romantic by virtue of our critical methodologies and their founding metaphysics.[10] To say this is not to challenge Christensen's excellent insight that our receptiveness to things Derridean mirrors Coleridge's embrace of Burke's solution to *his* legitimation crisis. Surely, Christensen is right to track today's valorized 'trace' and its political interests back to Burke's way of glamorizing the peculiar absence of the British Constitution. But to stop with that set of homologies and to cast it as a causal affair is to be incomplete to the point of error. We must look to the ways that the lives which produced those analogously deconstructive methods and values *themselves* got produced. We must ask, for example, whether the different but related crises of the Romantic and the postmodern ages – the crisis transition from agrarian to industrial capitalism, and, from industrial to multinational consumer capitalism – could begin to explain this strange mirroring. This is the *kind* of question that will, we think, illuminate our own (and the Romantics') Crisis mentality and our own (and the Romantics') tendency to equate criticism with 'intervention'. (In passing, I note that these two facts of our intellectual life are crucial components of the new historicism.) More important, such questions may suggest how those facts – episodes in an epic of the Kantian Subject, powerful to know his incapacity to Know, his gift to *transcend* that understanding in the 'reflecting judgement' of art – serve the system they think to undo.

Returning to a more limited question of method, let me note that each of our essays demonstrates its abhorrence of the mill. We hope to produce a distinct critical process in response to and by way of engendering the workings of each item we study. We would not consider it a compliment to be described (as a colleague of mine recently praised a guest speaker) as 'so well positioned' that no question, no example, could throw us off balance. We would like, I think, to *lose* our balance as a result of the changes we institute in the works we study. For each object, a new action; and with each action, ultimately, a *newer* object emerging and of course, a changed subject position too.

We may take as the covering phrase for these critical vicissitudes one of the rubrics from Wallace Stevens's ur- and ultra-Romantic poem, 'Notes Toward a Supreme Fiction'. To say 'It Must Change' is to name a criticism that undergoes change – rewrites itself – in its changeful operations upon its object. Here, as in the essay that follows, I invoke Stevens's headings – the commandments of this *particular* authority – in order to indicate my investment in my Romantic subject. Whatever truth gets told by my reading will be a function of that investment, as of the distance and difference which are its founding statutes. It occurs to me now that each of the pieces in this collection is, similarly, organized by Stevens's threefold directive, and that this is a good lesson for today.

> It Must Be Abstract
> It Must Change
> It Must Give Pleasure

By his phrase, 'And see the sun . . . clearly in the idea of it', Stevens names an act of ideation whereby the sun and the seer are made to focus each other in their identical/incommensurable fields. Stevens would like to persuade us that the subject–object positions which are his, and our, Romantic inheritance do not survive this operation. To propose for our criticism an abstracting move – a detour through concepts – is not just to refuse the idea of a textual or historical object, patiently awaiting formalist (empirical *or* deconstructive) description. It is to articulate that mutually estranging, mutually constitutive project sketched above. The detouring concept need not be a theoretical construct; it may, as in Butler's work, take the form of a period and/or genre idea (for example, the Enlightenment progress poem).

In the practice of *any* kind of historicism – new or new-critical – that interchangeably authored critique I describe entails, first, a statement of the rationale motivating one's selection of illuminative contexts. Second, it involves a refashioning of those contexts according to their corrosive effects upon one's primary text. The juxtaposition of five different discursive categories – repetitions in diverse tones of one's study text – will not magically engender a sixth and a critical thing. Nor do we avoid the perils of a positivist idealism simply by privileging a 'discourse' over a 'fact', and certainly not by *conflating* discourse with facts, texts with contexts, and literature with politics. Each period has its way of relating these categories. To homogenize them is to annihilate the very object of one's criticism, the modes of relation, and to indenture oneself to their ghosts. Fredric Jameson advanced this caution a long time ago, but it still bears rehearsing.[11] In these essays, we try to avoid the post-structuralist pitfall as well as the more obvious, mimetic danger. Echoing McGann's rich repetition, we do not devote ourselves to either beauty, the one of inflection or the one of innuendo: the blackbird whistling or just after.[12] To describe our work as a reflected rather than referential criticism is to mark its departure from the allegorical approaches common in much new historicist work and, from the symbolic-organic readings fast on their way to defining a 'new materialism'. Not one of our essays sets up an extra-textual item – a figure of historical immediacy – as the origin or explanation of a discursive double. Nor do the authors of this book equate the concrete incoherences and binary reversals of the deconstructed text with an irreducible, subversive 'bodiliness', a textual 'carnivalesque'. We are of the mind that every theme – history, the body, self-consciousness – once it is granted singular subject-status, vanishes into its own clouds of glory. Quite right.

In our essays, a concept of the historical object will be found to accompany and disturb whatever gets positioned through our reconstructions as the empirical thing itself. In our visibly constructed knowledge of the things we study, we confess our distance from the lived interior of those things, from *meaning*. The reader of McGann's essay will find this confession both in the imaginative selection of study texts (the concatenation of the *Oresteia*, Blake's *Milton* and Pound's *Cantos*) and, as in Marilyn Butler's essay, in the patient exposition of those minute particulars which these two remarkable scholars so skilfully produce. Both authors vex the archival authority of their work by a stylistically signalled distinction between 'archives' – a fetishized form of the past – and a past so thoroughly mediated as to make it, for those who first *made* it, entirely unmediated. 'The natives of the rain are rainy men.' Neither Butler nor McGann, for all their confidence in a knowable past and in their instruments of knowledge, aspires towards native understanding. By adding concrete details to our pictures of the past, and by adding to the least likely, least *designated* of places, both writers (like Stevens himself, the author of that drily distanced observation above) alter the largest structures of our received views. For McGann and Butler, the point of this alteration is political. For Butler, the salient question is that of canon formation, or what gets taught and how in Thatcher's England. McGann's abiding question comes to him through Benjamin and Fanon. That question – really, an *injunction* to probe the relation of culture to barbarism in and through every document we study – is also, implicitly, Butler's. The procedural and rhetorical difference you will mark in McGann's work (the immediate, *ad hominem* and morally urgent way he *puts* his question), will suggest his different – in some ways more Romantic and definitely more narrativized – concept of politics.

Paul Hamilton's essay, like my own, names the circumstanced nature of its truths by its obvious concern with current critical practice, a pragmatic interest, and by its frankly arranged marriage of philosophy to material life, with poetry acting as go-between. The reader will find this essay marked by a metaphysical wit operating at the level of argument, not discourse. Or, speaking technically now, we *could* describe Hamilton's analytic method as a wit of tropes – displacement – so long as we follow him in recognizing displacement as the very condition as well as the mechanism of knowledge.

Furthermore, and as I've been arguing, the ages are always yoked together by violence. Arnold's Hellenes and Hebrews, securely distributed between creative and critical ages, are a fiction of what never was. Hamilton's wit is not, then, a matter of unnatural couplings between diverse historical and formal categories (viz. Keats and Adorno, script and scrip, Mammon and 'the Monastry', poetry and 'the Police'). Rather, it is Johnson's *second* definition of wit that is adumbrated by Hamilton's essay: that which articulates relations so just (so foundational, that is) as to have escaped observation altogether. And, lest we imagine that we are the first to find out the tautology in the word 'anachronism', we should turn to Wordsworth, whose every line betrays his knowledge that all of our moments are defined by their containment of the times they are not. Hamilton's essay and my own dramatize the role reversal forever at work within our historical experience. Our Hellenes (Keats, Wordsworth) are given to strangely Hebraic interests, and we Hebrews imitate the Hellenic inflection.

A criticism 'gives pleasure' when it refuses the illusory difference of a subject-or-object centred critique: that is, the choice between a privileging of function (the uses of the past: a presentist, pragmatist project) or of being (the patient essence of the past: an archaeology not of knowledge but of meaning). A pleasure-giving criticism restores the doubleness that Lacan has named the Imaginary. Through such a discourse, we settle for a moment on the surface of the mirroring past. Here, we encounter an image of a self that, in its distance and difference from our present interior, is precisely *not* a self. At the same time, this image, in offering a totalized form of our historical self – a coherent version of our otherwise centrifugal sensations – brings into being that self 'in itself', and into *future* being, a 'for itself'.

Dominick LaCapra, in a version of a lecture he gave at the University of Pennsylvania last year, concludes his searching critique of the new historicism by proposing the Freudian notion of transference as a model for today's historically oriented criticisms. My own outline of a discourse which renders its transformative, subject-site undecidable might be read as a diachronic version of the contained vicissitudes LaCapra marks out.

> The concept of transference offers an alternative to historicism and presentism in understanding the historian's relation to the past . . . At the very least the notion of transference helps to illuminate the prevalent feeling among historians that in their work they develop an intimate relation to their material and to other students of it – a relation that is not adequately accounted for in standard notions of objectivity or subjectivity, manipulation of data or empathy.[13]

LaCapra observes the dynamics of transference in a number of institutional situations. For our purposes, the most interesting is the transference which obtains 'in the relation of the historian to the "object" of study'.

> Transference in this . . . more general and perhaps more basic sense refers to the manner in which the problems at issue in the object of study reappear (or are repeated with variations) in the work of the historian. It also indicates the problem of understanding temporality in terms of a process of repetition with change . . . in contrast to the standard binary oppositions between the universal and the particular, permanence and change, continuity and discontinuity.[14]

What transference substitutes for those 'standard binary oppositions' is a 'complex repetitive temporality'. By that phrase, La Capra invokes Freud's notion of the way in which the very *originality* of an event – its status *as* an event in a psychic narrative (that is, as traumatic) and as *originary*, in the sense of engendering and, thus, explanatory – is constituted retrospectively both through its 'real life' repetition and, in a third phase, by the displaced repetition precipitated through the analysis. We must be very clear on the fact that what is 'constituted retrospectively' really exists, not in the ho-hum order of present narration (the order, that is, of intersubjective, discursive facticity), but in the historical medium itself, the temporal record. LaCapra's ideal historian is a prophet who, in looking backwards and seeing the past clearly in the idea of it, changes that past's future, the present. In that selfsame instant, he revises the past and his *own* future into alignment with that newly invented but also predestined future/present. In the sub-title of the essay that follows, I gloss this riddle by the phrase 'back to the future'. The better gloss is, of course, the plot of the movie that wears that title. To believe in this 'complex repetitive temporality' is to begin speaking of the analytic narrative – of history, that is – as a reconstruction, as prophecy and as invention without contradiction.

It is interesting to recall in this context a distinction McGann worked out a few years back. In *The Romantic Ideology*, McGann defines repetition as the non-normative way in which poetry reproduces ideology. Reification, conversely, names the abstract and systematic way in which ideology gets fetishized. We bring this formal distinction into LaCapra's dynamic account by way of

Freud's concept of 'poised attention'. This is the name for that free-floating, non-systematic listening which, in allowing for 'the play of the analyst's unconscious in responding to the analysand', provides access to phenomena 'that would [otherwise] have a meaning only *nachtraglich* if at all'.[15] LaCapra locates the special objectivity of the transference relation in this attitude.

It would seem that the distinctively non-logical discourse half-created by the analyst's 'poised attention' is just what McGann calls 'repetition'. Interestingly, both McGann and LaCapra relate this disorganized language, or its truth-value, to Bakhtin's 'dialogism', which they understand not as some kind of harmonious intersubjectivity (that is, 'dialogue'), but rather as the cleavages opened between conscious and unconscious *within* the historian/analyst and his subject/patient; and also, *between* the unconsciousness of analyst and patient, critic and poet, present and past.[16] In these divides are found the opportunities for acts of relation. These acts do not, in Wordsworth's phrase, 'heal the breach'. Following McGann, they do not conduce to 'power', or a literature thereof, but rather to knowledge.[17] McGann believes that knowledge, or science in the form of repetition – an irreducibly human, concrete and situated (re)production of ideology – is what distinguishes poetry from all the other mediations. It is also what he himself embraces in his critical desideratum, the 'picture of great detail'. What LaCapra does not need to spell out but what we, with our special academic circumstances, do, is that transference as any kind of critical model includes, and always included, so-called 'counter-transference'. Without that practical error – the pressure of the human, concrete, non-systematic – as part of the interpretative manner and means, there would be no truth. To return to the psychoanalytic model, criticism comes by its insights through the exaggerated and formalized alienation of the relationship between analyst and patient – a spatial distance – and the metaphysical absurdity of its reconstructive, temporal project. To consider this absurdity an *obstacle* to the historical venture would be like viewing the analyst's distance from the analysand as a hindrance to their work. All of us who try to read the past are in similarly narrow rooms. The prison is in pretending to be uncircumstanced, in aspiring to identity.

The truth of poetry is a moving form. One cannot say that art is or is not one of the ideologies, for it all depends on when you catch it: Blake would say, in which 'state'. 'What was once imagined is now believed' does not, I think, describe a continuous and conservative journey towards transparency. It does not, that is, describe historicism as either the nineteenth or the late twentieth century knows those practices. Nor is Blake's proverb a version of Shelley's exhortation to imagine what we know, for Blake would find that an impossible project unless addressed to audiences separated by vast reaches of time (or, to psyches operating in a fourfold, and, dialectical fashion). What was once imagined because it was too close for knowing – because it was the very apparatus that made science possible – was the deep truth of that age: that which resists symbolization absolutely. Blake, a Christian and merciful poet, tells us in all his prophetic poems that these abstract imaginings will, in time, acquire determinate form. Belief is Blake's name for those saving incarnations. They are error, the error that, the scientists tell us, conditions the truth-value of our propositions. But, because they are also the origin, explanation and effect of the present age's imaginings – *its* non-symbolized, its non-normative, its anti-knowledge – they are also truth.

As a final remark introductory to this collection, let me note that each of our authors, persons very much within the Anglo-American academy, will be found to pronounce his or her ambivalence towards absorption by the structures that give us our voice. Consistent with the argument outlined above, the ambivalence we express and that which we accomplish are not at all identical. Still, we hope that in the very tension and conflict at work within each essay and among them, a resistance we cannot conceive, much less execute, might begin to take shape. I quote from Jean-François Lyotard's answer to the question, 'what is postmodernism?': 'our business is not to supply reality but to invent allusions to the conceivable which cannot be presented.'[18] Lyotard reminds us that this business of yoking the concept to its non-representation was precisely the office of Kant's sublime. This is to say, he too locates the postmodern – something evermore about to be – in the Romantic age.

Notes

1. Edward Pechter, 'The New Historicism and its Discontents: Politicizing Renaissance Drama', *PMLA*, vol. 102, no. 3 (May 1987), pp. 292–303, p. 292.
2. Ibid., p. 292.
3. Marilyn Butler, 'Revising the Canon', *Times Literary Supplement*, 4–10 December 1987.
4. 'The argument that art works are independent of the artist sounds like a delusional version of *l'art pour l'art*. It is not. It is a simple expression of the more complex idea that art is defined by its relation to a society governed by the law of objectification: it is only *qua* things that art works become the antithesis of the reified social order. Linked to this is the fact that *works of art, and that includes the so-called individualistic ones, speak the language of a "We", not of an "I", and they do so to the extent to which they refrain from conforming in some extrinsic fashion to that "We" and its idiom*' (emphasis mine), Theodor Adorno, *Aesthetic Theory*, trans. C. Lenhardt (London: Routledge & Kegan Paul, 1984), p. 240.
5. I thank Jacqueline Rose for this description of Margaret Thatcher's intellectual style, and for her analytic insights into the surprising popularity of that style. 'Margaret Thatcher and Ruth Ellis', Conference on Criticism and Materialism, University of Colorado, Spring 1988.
6. Quoted in Theodor Adorno, *Against Epistemology: a Metacritique, Studies in Husserl and the Phenomenological Antinomies*, trans. W. Domingo (Cambridge, Mass.: MIT Press, 1983), p. 5.
7. Jerome McGann, 'Poetic Ideology and Nonnormative Truth', pp. 73–94, in *Social Values and Poetic Acts: the Historical Judgment of Literary Work* (Cambridge, Mass.: Harvard University Press, 1988).
8. Philippe Lacoue-Labarthe and Jean-Luc Nancy, *The Literary Absolute*, trans. P. Barnard and C. Lester (Albany, NY: State University of New York Press, 1988), pp. 16, 17.
9. Dominick LaCapra, 'Intellectual History and Critical Theory', in *The New Philosophy of History*, ed. Frank Ankersmit and Hans Kellner, forthcoming (cited from manuscript).
10. Jerome Christensen, '"Like a Guilty Thing Surprised": Deconstruction, Coleridge, and the Apostasy of Criticism', *Critical Inquiry*, vol. 12, no. 4 (Summer 1986), pp. 769–87.
11. Fredric Jameson, 'Marxism and Historicism', *New Literary History*, 1979.
12. 'I do not know which to prefer, / The beauty of inflections / Or the beauty of innuendoes, / The blackbird whistling / Or just after.' Wallace Stevens, 'Thirteen Ways of Looking at a Blackbird', quoted as epigraph by McGann, *The Beauty of Inflections: Literary Investigations in Historical Method and Theory*, (Oxford and New York: Oxford University Press, 1985).
13. LaCapra, 'Intellectual History'.
14. Ibid.
15. Ibid.
16. My word 'disorganized' alludes on the slant to Shelley's word 'organized'.

[The poets'] language is vitally metaphorical; that is, it marks the before unapprehended relations of things and perpetuates their apprehension, until the words which represent them become, through time, signs for portions or classes of thought instead of pictures of integral thoughts; and then, if no new poets should arise to create afresh the associations which have been thus disorganized, language will be dead to all the nobler purposes of human intercourse. (from 'A Defence of Poetry')

Like Shelley, McGann distinguishes the way in which poetry, as opposed to all the other mediations, puts ideology in play, by reference to its irreducibly 'pictural', concrete character. Similarly, McGann follows Shelley in regarding the traditionally 'organized' discourses – the abstract orders: law, theology, philosophy, etc. – as mystifications. In so far as these systems hide the structures or *organon* of material life and its modes of production – in that they disguise the incommensurabilities that poetry thematizes – they are themselves 'disorganized' and are also forces for disorganization.

The point of this note is to demonstrate the presence of the Romantic ideology in the very language of this critique and of McGann's. In *representing* the echo – materially reproducing the relation inscribed in our practice – we change one term in that relation, altering thereby the relation itself and, thus, changing the first term too.

17 McGann, Introduction to the Clark Lectures, Cambridge, 1988 (cited from manuscript).
18 Jean-François Lyotard, *The Postmodern Condition*, trans. G. Bennington and B. Massumi (Minneapolis: University of Minnesota Press, 1984), p. 81.

1

The New Historicism: Back to the Future

Marjorie Levinson

I

We have seen within Romantic studies over the past five years a new zeal to position literary works within a historical domain. More dramatically, many of us use that domain to identify and interrogate the work's representational choices. The enthusiasm attending this 'new historicist' investigation marks our sense of emancipation. We trust to our contextual and retextualizing procedures to put us beyond the interpretative norms imposed by the poetry and sanctified by the most influential of this century's criticism of that poetry.

In light of these interests and attitudes, the name we have given our critical practice executes a Freudian slip of the first order. By the word 'historicism' – a repetition of a nineteenth-century coinage – we confess our share in the very fictions we claim to de-mystify. Let me add another twist to this irony by suggesting that it is precisely our interest in the Romantic ideology – I shall say, its interest in us – that puts us in position to elucidate and transvalue the poetry of the early nineteenth century. We are, in short, situated to read that literature dialectically.

This business of interest is a question of historical conjunctures, not enthusiasm. Or, 'enthusiasm' will do so long as we construe it as a dynamic response to objective relations. The immediate distinction between today's interest and the relatively sustained study of the Romantics conducted throughout most of this century is the widespread, spontaneous and, by its account, non-strategic revaluation now under way in the academy. Eliot's devaluation, an isolated campaign, was largely a tactical manoeuvre determined by his revaluation on behalf of another literature, that of the sixteenth and early seventeenth centuries. Moreover, the entire literary discussion was plainly advanced as an exercise in contemporary social instruction. Yale's influential seriousness aligned itself early on with a theoretical project. This, we might say, was the effective interest of its philosophic and formal operation upon the Romantic canon. Certainly, Eliot's depreciation and Yale's appreciation can and should be read as dynamic reflections of social change and as part of the field which includes the poetry in question. Today's criticism differs in its untheorized and unselfconsciously political situation. This gives it a special place – a place privileged, ironically, by the kind and extent of its possession by the object it studies. The special intelligence of this criticism will come from its opportunity to investigate its object within the terrain of subjective knowledge and practice.[1]

There are the meanings you choose, and then there are the meanings that choose you. In the case of our new historicism, one can discern at least four orders of determination, only two of which will I elaborate in this essay.[2] Before I begin that account, let me characterize the project to which it contributes as a reading of a body of work produced over the past five years, a corpus that includes my own studies.[3] Since I hope to discover what is entailed by our practice, mine will be a highly generalizing representation of a wide range of critical work. I think many of us are curious about the meaning of our interest and anxious to see how we can best pursue it now, in light of our recent experience. I hope this curiosity will allow for the necessarily reductive way I shall conduct this inquiry. Let me also observe that my topic is that new historicism which has emerged within Romantic studies. I say 'our' historicism to distinguish this critical endeavour from that movement in Renaissance studies associated with Stephen Greenblatt, Louis Montrose, Frank Whigham, and others.

The new historicism – a direct assault upon Yale's present-mindedness and an attempt to surpass the extrinsic and binary contextualism of twentieth-century scholarship – has emerged as a kind of systems analysis, an approach that, by its very form, indicates yet a third critical target.[4] By our functionalist exercises in closed-field intertextuality, we tacitly reject that teleological formalism associated with the old historicism, the dominant form of nineteenth-century historiography. Ours is an empirically responsible investigation of the contemporary meanings informing literary works (their parts, their production, their reception), as well as other social texts.[5] We regard these meanings as systematically interrelated within the period in question, but since we do not organize the system by a dynamic concept of ideology on the one hand, and of structural determination on the other, our inquiries do not give rise to a meaningful historical sequence. In the absence of some such model of epochal relatedness, questions concerning our own critical interest cannot materialize. By suppressing such questions, we do not, as we think, *surpass* the old historicism with its providential coherences and one-way dialectics, we install it at the heart of our practice. It is precisely our failure to articulate a critical field that sights *us* even as we compose *it*, that brings back the positivism, subjectivism and relativism of the rejected historicist methodology.

Where our historicism genuinely surpasses its nineteenth-century namesake is in its adoption of some specifically Marxian critical methods and values. Our interest in motivating *objectively* the special differences of Romantic works and responses – like our sensitivity to their contradictions and discontinuities – is a Marxian emphasis and a real departure from both the empiric formalism and the gradualism of Romantic historiography. Where we fall back into the received Romantic field is in our failure, first, to objectify our own subjectivity (that is, our way of *producing* that value), and second, to articulate the subject–object, present–past, criticism–poetry polarities as a mode of relation. As it is, we seem determined *not* to make anything of the historical differentials precipitated by our criticism.

One important corollary of this restraint is our failure to *represent* the critical practice which, by its cross-referencing, relates phenomena that were, in the past's immanent and differentiated experience of itself, either not related, differently related or unselfconsciously related. *We* are the ones who, by putting the past to a certain use, put it in a certain order. While most of us know this, we seem not to consider that this interest of ours in a certain use might also be an *effect* of the past which we study, and that our mode of critical production could be related to that past as to the absent cause which our practice instantiates. What I'm describing is a specifically *transhistorical* dialectic, one that invents the critic as Schlegel's prophet looking backwards.

By thinking along these lines, we learn to manage some basic hermeneutic binds. Here is Tony Bennett (who, for today's historicists, is the likelier influence than Stanley Fish, the larger and more stationary target of this critique), on the task which faces Marxist criticism. This task is not, Bennett says,

> that of reflecting or bringing to light the politics which is already there, as a latent presence within the text which has to be made manifest. It is that of actively politicizing the text, of making its politics for it, by producing a new position for it within the field of cultural relations and, thereby, new forms of use and effectivity within the broader social process.[6]

This kind of thinking (in the text [essentialism]/outside the text [pragmatism]: passive reflecting, elucidating/active politicizing, use) is predialectical and therefore not the task of a Marxist or any other criticism today. Bennett's either/or formulation puts us in fact in a single box: namely, a privileging of the text's original or its most belated position. If we choose *not* to rehearse the politics produced for the work by the way it got written and, initially, read, then we must crisply depose the authority of first things, which is to say, we transfer that authority to last or latest things. This use-value pragmatism, which cordons off from criticism the present, or its special modes of cultural consumption, describes as well a commodity concept of literature. It imagines a work capable of dissolving the traces of its production and its history of receptions. The proposition that we can in any simple sense 'make a poem's politics for it' is also a definition of a text which descends – or rather, ascends – to us as a pure form. If essentialism is the danger of the first option, relativism and formalism are the perils of the second. Interestingly, historicism proper (the nineteenth-century variety) resolves in practice into this particular, and illusory, Scylla and Charybdis.

We want to articulate the literatures of the past in such a way as to accommodate the contingency of the present – the wilfulness of our textual politics – and at the same time, to configurate that freedom with the particular past that is retextualized. We want a framework that will explain the objective value of a belated criticism, one which reads into the work anticipations that were *not* present in the text's contemporary life, only in its posthumous existence, an existence that turns around and *plants itself* in the past. Within such a framework, today's criticism can assume its properly active, interested, 'subject' role and simultaneously figure as part of the objective field which includes the work: its original political position and its reception history.

Of course, to articulate this framework means giving up our notion of time as something different from histories (of matter, we might say, as something different from energy). It means conceiving the epochal distinctiveness of Romantic poetry not, chiefly, as a function of natural and therefore monolithic temporality, but as a result of determinate differences obtaining between the productive formations of the early nineteenth century and the late twentieth century, of the different ideological tasks defined by those formations, and finally, of the diverse kinds or levels of relatedness which those basic differences establish.

Our embrace of the Marxian methodology is a delicately selective affair and it is also a rejection of the Marxian content, or of the synoptic imperative which is the law of that content. Our reluctance to relate ourselves by difference to the objects we study is an attempt to save the present and its subjectivity from objectification by a critically transformed past. With a predictable irony, our conscientiously heterodox empiricism – our refusal to *repeat* the Romantic form of knowledge: literally, a refusal of the narrative principle that governs romance – locates our freedom within the mythic, untransformed past we have taken such pains to dismantle. Indeed, our discreetly truncated dialectics construct that particular myth all over again. We have, in short, and very much against our will, reified the Romantic science.

Let me put a happier accent on this irony and at the same time establish the character of my own interest in the subject. I have suggested that in some respects, our new and scandalous criticism is a reprise of our critical object: the Romantic ideology. I have also implied, however, that a world – or worlds – of difference separates the original from its reproduction. (More specifically, 'the alienation of the objectified result is not the same as the alienation at the point of departure. It is the passage from one to the other that defines [the subject].')[7] We may characterize our new historicism as that 'thought which is lost and alienated in the course of [the] action so that it may be rediscovered by and in the action itself'.[8] To say this – to quote Sartre in this context – is a way of suggesting that our consciousness of Romantic poetry is the consciousness *of* that practice ('of' in the genitive sense) produced as a moment in the course of its accomplishment. We use the fact of our interest, then, to plot our position within the objective field radiating from or including both the object we study and the existence we create for ourselves (the future we project for ourselves) by that study. Since our critical practice has already figured 1798 and 1988 – or certain sectors of those formations – as part of a developing, leap-frogging totalization, we have no choice but to study this phenomenon. By 'totalization' – which is here Sartre's word – I mean to describe a structure that comes into being only through the dialectical practice of the present, which is read as the delayed effect of that structure. We define the structure of the past as an absent cause promoting a range of effects that, at a certain historical moment, configurate with an origin to which they are related by difference and distance. At that moment – which we regard as a unique opportunity for critical translation – the origin coalesces as a structure, one which is really, suddenly, there in the past, but only by the retroactive practice of the present. Our totalizing act thus becomes part of the movement by which history continually reorganizes itself. Even as we wait upon the real development of that history as the sufficient condition for our critical acts, these acts also hasten that development. This is to say that we really *are* part of the object we study, subject to the changes that our study effects.[9]

I will return to this puzzling figure of a history that runs, in the idiom of today, 'back to the future'.[10] For now, let's consider the most complex and least explored of the semantic domains informing another recent phrase, 'new historicism'. Our resistance to Yale, our revision of contextual scholarship and our Marxian borrowings are the meanings *we* have chosen. I address the old historicism – that order of meaning which has chosen us – because by its very situation outside our critical reflections, it overdetermines the whole field of our practice.

I cannot undertake an analytic description of that historicism – partly for lack of space but also because the works that descend to us under that rubric have so little in common in the way of positive practice. They share certain negative determinations, or evince on the whole a consistently reactive interest in the historiography of the Enlightenment. But with respect to narrative means, manner and end, Ranke and Dilthey – to take the most dramatic examples – are not easily located in the same universe. Moreover, historicism has been so variously interpreted in the different disciplines and by intellectuals representing so many institutions and spanning so many moments, that to attempt a generic description would be, clearly, a fiction – not necessarily of what never *was*, but what is certainly at this point, *not*. Nor, given the focus of this paper, is there much point in developing a sequence of practical descriptions. Wesley Morris introduces his *Toward a New Historicism* with a lucid, schematic survey of the main definitions of historicism and he identifies some recurrent thematic elements as well. Hans Meyerhoff's *The Philosophy of History in our Time* has a good introduction and a useful selection of excerpts. I also refer the reader to J. C. D. Clark's *English Society: 1688–1832* for its opening discussion of the Whig interpretation of history, a historicist doctrine, and for its representation of the debate surrounding that doctrine.[11] (Both the doctrine and the debate are of special interest to students of the nineteenth century.) What is common to most accounts of historicism is its emphasis on change, subjectivism and continuity. Following Althusser, historicism is the belief that history has a subject and a telos.[12]

Hayden White groups the master historicists by reference to their discursive procedures: specifically, their substitution of representation itself in the form of emplotment, for argument as an explanatory strategy.[13] In his discussion of the ideological postures historicism has assumed vis-à-vis the historical field, and, at a more primary level, its diverse prefigurations of the field as a domain susceptible to particular linguistic protocols, White provides a wealth of comparative analysis, enormously suggestive for today's Romanticists.

Because, however, we want to articulate the *form* of relation obtaining between historicism, Romanticism and today's new historicism, I propose that rather than analyse methods and themes, we configurate our topics around that philosophical crux which was the explicit problematic of Romantic poetry, the transition in this critical argument. It is my feeling that both historicism and Romanticism were, among other things, solutions to an abstract problem possessed of a definite political salience in the period. If we can understand the meaning of that problem, we might discover why its solution should still be with us in the different but related mode of our new historicism. Since it is our own critical practice that concerns us here, and because we want to get at this by analysing the working self-consciousness of the Romantic canon, I restrict my account to the realm of practical, as opposed to philosophic history. What gets dropped, then, or rather shunted to the subtext of this essay, is Hegel.

The model I propose – a more reductive one than most – sandwiches Romanticism and historicism, conceived as comparable functional responses, between Enlightenment materialism on the one side, and Marx's dialectically historical materialism on the other.[14]

We begin by isolating the logical problem of Enlightenment materialism: an abstract, essentialist doctrine. By 'problem', I mean the emergence of this doctrine, through the vicissitudes of the Revolutionary era, as a Cartesian affair. The materialism of the eighteenth century was, we recall, the Revolutionary, demotic, identity principle. Cartesian idealism, the difference principle, provided the *ancien régime its* onto-epistemological model.[15] Elsewhere, I've argued that by 1805, Wordsworth (whom I shall use as a Romantic instance) had come to recognize in his own Cartesian opportunisms the identity of Reason in its most and least exalted moods: synecdochically, Imagination and Napoleon.[16] The mind that keeps its own inviolate retirement from the object world, which it knows by negation, and the mind that, essentially identified with matter, knows no resistance to its ambitious negativity, are one and the same. A matter that doesn't exist in any necessary way for mind cannot in any necessary way affect it. Literally, what you don't know can't hurt you. Then again, a matter conceived as mind's alter ego forfeits its practical authority over thought, the prerogative of that which, by resisting my desires, constitutes me as their bearer and thus as a distinctively human subject. The figure of the contemplative Cartesian philosopher joins the Napoleonic figure in their mutual denial of the determining instance of matter.[17] The flip side of this denial is, of course, the postulate of a non-contingent subject and its perfect command of reality.

We may characterize this subject a bit more fully by tracing out the abstract, purely *formal* imbrication of the Cartesian and materialist positions. Basically, we want to observe that an abstract materialism necessarily posits a consciousness at once immaterial and structurally self-alienated. We recall that while Cartesian idealism knows nothing of the physical world, Enlightenment materialism knows everything pertaining to matter: which is to say, everything there is, with one exception. It cannot know the knowledge produced by matter. Were the individual to *think* his essential materiality (his consciousness, that is), thought would become different from its object, its operations mechanically reflexive. Self-consciousness is thus constituted – by default, as it were – as negative matter: an essential *différance*, if we can allow that solecism for a moment. Similarly, although materialism produces, as by its founding statute, complete working knowledge of the world, it also, in so far as it conceives that domain as locus of the Real, confers upon the consciousness *of* that knowledge the form of glimpses, gods, concepts: that is, representations. This is because objective knowledge that knows itself as such must, by the laws of materialism, mean conscious coincidence with its object. Immediate, intelligent identity with essential matter is only conceivable if matter is already 'in motion': already a form of consciousness.

The interesting paradox, then, of the materialist position is its way of producing the very concepts that undo it. I refer both to the idea of knowing as, ultimately, a dissociated, conceptual activity, and to the idea of consciousness as absolute negativity. The postulate of matter as an essential Real engenders the idea of the subject as owner of concepts precipitated by and consisting of matter-in-motion but hopelessly alienated from the deep truth of matter-at-rest. This last is, of course, a metaphysical presence conjured by a doctrine which, by designating matter in a fashion at once absolute and mechanical, deposits in its diverse forms (external and internal) an essential, unknowable quality. To follow Enlightenment materialism to its necessary end is to wind up in that familiar Romantic, and also Cartesian place: a world that is not our own and, much more, not ourselves and therefore nothing *but* the hum of thoughts evaded in the mind.

To frame this paradox more topically is also to read in the practical collapse of those polar, intellectual positions the breakdown of the mythic social extremes they denoted. Neither 'the people' nor 'the aristocracy' – those moving forms – could survive the Cartesian–materialist slippage. What emerged in the Napoleonic form (a class term in both senses) was a single guilty hero: the absolute bourgeois. The reading of the Revolution as a dialectical agon between high and low – prolific contraries – gave way to the image of an unopposed, and therefore sterile negation pursuing its juggernaut career. In other words, the special subject form defined by the high–low, Cartesian–materialist complicities we have discussed (namely: the idea of an agent as productively estranged from his own consciousness as from the world it invests) took as its historical content Napoleon, itself the form of a new social content: the middle class.

Just very roughly, let's situate this image – the mark of a charged categorical contamination – in a dynamic social field. We recall the project of the early nineteenth-century middle class: not just to make itself but to make itself into an *essentially* self-making class. Such a class would naturally wish to establish a more honoured position for a transformative materialism ('humanization', to use the Romantic word) than the Cartesian system afforded. What was rejected in the *cogito* was the static and organic social norm it inscribed. At the same time, the essentialist Cartesian distinction between matter and mind, objects and concepts, would have to be maintained – indeed, reinforced – if the ascent of a class from its position as object of a superior consciousness to a subject in its own right and vis-à-vis its objectification of the lower orders were to mean anything. To secure its positional identity, the middle class had to install a permanent, structural difference between its own subjectivity and the object status of the class below it. It had to devise, in short, a model of one-way, end-stopped transformation if it were to avoid deconstruction by the imitative ascent of the lower orders.

By reference to this project – the mirror-image of the Napoleonic adventure – the sign of Napoleon constituted a terrible threat. In that sign, the age might decipher not just the fraudulence of the Enlightenment's Cartesian contestation and thus the fundamental error of the Revolution, but the material, class-specific expedience of that error.

The job of the middle class – enacted through, among many other strategies, the doctrines we call Romanticism and historicism – was to remotivate the categorical chiasmus that history itself, in the form of Napoleon, had effected. The practical task of this class was the rehabilitation of the self-made maker idea, a concept essential to its project and gravely endangered by its association with the Napoleonic *Bildungsroman*. Historicism conceived for the purposes of its redemptive mission a new materialism, which we can call a historical and a dialectical materialism, but *not* a historically dialectical materialism.

What was 'material' about historicism was its insistence upon the immanent reality and meaning of historical phenomena: this, however, and rather confusingly, a function of their essentially subjective character. Enlightenment historiography had characterized such events as epiphenomenal: by-products of the self-determining activity of an abstract principle, Reason, operating within a historical field clotted with ignorance and superstition. Historicism, concerned to establish the dignity and autonomy of (class)-historical experience, countered the tyranny of an extrinsic, abstract absolutism with an intrinsic authority: namely, mind, conceived at a very high level of abstraction and as the source of history's special materiality. For historicism, the reality and meaning of historical life are aligned with its capacity to be dissolved back into consciousness, or *im*materialized.[18]

What made historicism 'dialectical', and also so very startling an event in intellectual history, was its articulation of history's present –past problematic along philosophy's subject–object axis. Like Descartes, historicism asserts that we cannot in any immediate and certain way know the object – the past – as it is: which is to say, *was*. We can, however, use our consciousness to *cure* the past of its objectivity: in effect, its pastness. We can do this because all that is properly called 'history' was originally and is *essentially* a form of subjectivity objectified by our temporal remove. This discovery of the human character of the historiographic object was, of course,

Vico's great accomplishment. History, then, unlike Holbach's matter, Descartes' objects and Vico's Nature, is a human product: to turn materialism's key phrase, motion-in-matter. As such, or in this form, history can be known by us. The historian's first task, then, is to establish the intelligibility of the past by restoring it to its original subjective state, either by an empathic re-enactment or through an engagement with the less objectified forms of the historical record: what we today would call material and popular culture. Humanized, the past lives, moves and has its being again but differently – on a higher level – in the present. We can recognize in this quintessentially historicist process Coleridge's – one should say, Hegel's – act of self-consciousness diachronically staged: the subject *makes* itself a subject by constructing itself objectively to itself, in the process, realizing its object.

We might notice one large difference between the Hegelian paradigm and the narratives it authorized: a difference largely concealed by the appropriately objective concerns of a historiography classically conceived. In practice, the historian's production of the past does not in any way re-produce *him* or his agency. The present is edified but not *changed* by its scholarly operations. Its subject-position remains intact – indeed, enhanced. By its failure to historicize the subjectivity of the present – to submit its consciousness to a critical objectification by the past – historicism not only violated its avowedly dialectical logic, it produced an abstract humanism which it called materialism. We have a model, in short, of one-way transformation masquerading as a dialectic.

We may glimpse in just this very schematic account of historicism's intellectual method a sort of mythic solution to the conflictual causality and action issues (as we've seen, social and economic issues), foregrounded by the Revolution. While we observe, for example, in historicism's transitive cognition an emphasis on practice as the distinguishing subject faculty, and on change as the distinctively human expression, we also remark the peculiarly passive, non-purposive and syncretic sort of change that historicism describes. Historicism could logically assert that knowledge, in so far as it irresistibly changes its object, *is* practice. At the same time, this sort of practice – effectivity without the embarrassments of alienation (desire, deliberation, execution) – is freedom, since the subject suffers no changes by its changeful operations. We have in this figure a sort of fantasy alternative to the consummate dialecticity of the Revolutionary drama: the emplotment of an action that consumed its origin, an effect that altered and displaced its cause. One might guess that the vigilant one-sidedness of historicism's dialectic enacts a defence against this narrative: the veritable archetype of a 'redundant energy, vexing its own creation'. At the same time, one discerns in the method a model for a peculiarly safeguarded exercise in social mobility.

In the annals of intellectual history, one regularly encounters allusions to something called the 'dilemma' of historicism. This seems to describe the bifurcation of historicist practice into an objective and subjective tendency. In light of the above discussion, one might focus this event as the separating out of those Cartesian and materialist elements that historicism had only held in suspension. In the objectively accented historicisms, the critical process (the restoration of the past to its subject-essence) is subordinated to the critical end: the objective truth of the past's subjectivity. In other words, the cardinal moment of historicist inquiry – the transformation of the past from an object into a subject, precondition to the exercise upon it of a positivist science – is elided. The historian of this temper (one thinks of Ranke) puts the present in the service of the past. His concern is the production of knowledge as if for its own sake, independent of its consequences for the present. ' . . . every age is immediate to God and . . . its value rests in no way upon what it produces but upon the very fact of its existence.' Ranke's often quoted statement brings out the danger, or extreme expression, of this objective historicism: its reduction of history to a meaningless array of facts. This is an absolute, as opposed to a contextual relativism, and that abstraction reinscribes what it thinks it refuses: namely, the absolute present. In this case, it is the scientific method that acts as privileged, essential subject.

On the other side – the side dominated by Dilthey – we find the assumption that one can know within or about the past only those data which originally pertained to the subject position, and even here, complete understanding is something longed for, never seen. (Objective life – an order of facticity experienced by its own age and the historian's as absolute, as *given* – does not enter into the field of this kind of inquiry. It is, in short, regarded as Nature rather than history.) The premise here is that because the subjectivity of the past is materially different from ours, it is *analytically* inaccessible. Hence the need for an object (phenomenal life as 'intended' by and in consciousness) and method (intuition) specific to the cultural sciences. Phenomenology is the name of this new discipline. Here, the critical process of reanimation assumes centre stage. In Ranke, this process is the preliminary exercise without which the scientific practice – the real business of historiography – could not proceed. In Dilthey, this metamorphosis of object to subject, past to present, *is* the practice. Dilthey's project, the (complementary) antithesis to Ranke's, is to make the past serve the present, or instruct its consciousness and practice. If the danger of Ranke's method is relativism, Dilthey's method risks an extreme subjectivism. Or, Ranke's historicism is organized by the principle of identity: and beyond that, by an underlying philosophic materialism. Dilthey's method is governed by the principle of difference; keeping with the configuration we've established, by a Cartesian model of consciousness and matter. We are back where we started.

I would like to put Marx in the breach opened by the 'dilemma of historicism'. His translation of historicism's essentialist dialectics into a historical form defined a metahistoricism whereby the dilemma was surpassed, its elements preserved but transfigured. Put in the simplest terms, Marx's great contribution to the historicist discourse was his demonstration that the subjectivity of the present, like that of the past, is objective; and, that this objectivity is at once absolute and historically, materially determined. Marx's dialectic, by historicizing historicism's constant – its essential present, or subject-position – cut out from under that doctrine its transhistorical transformational purchase and the liberal, abstract humanistic class logic which it entailed. Indeed, Marx not only refused a category of essential subjectivity, he allowed no essential human subject: no cause which is not reproduced by its effects. As we all know, his genius was to see that the past, restored to its objective subjectivity, swivels back upon the present and objectifies its good consciousness. The historian, the reader and the moment they share are all made strange to themselves, their freedom and natural necessity severely circumscribed.

Above, I characterized the Marxian objective domain as at once absolute and historically contingent. We explain this paradox by setting it against historicism's working concept of matter. As we observed, historicism's objective, material domain is either reducible to history proper – an immanent and essential subjectivity – or, it is Nature: the essentially given and, to the historian, impenetrable and uninteresting domain. In his engagement with history, the subject-historian alienates himself, but upon a medium with which he is *essentially* identified. (Kierkegaard isolates this logical bind in Hegel.) His detour through the past restores to that seeming object its early candour, which is also its deep truth and the historian's science. Because the historian 'recreates' or 'revives' the immanent subjectivity of the past – because he does not *produce* that value – his practice, while it enriches and enlightens him, leaves his dialectical position intact.

I rehearse this protocol so as to characterize its action curve. The movement described by historicism is continuous and syncretic, its hero the consciousness of the present.[19] What is missing, after the initial, easily surpassed present–past confrontation, is any representation of difference and contradiction: any *historically* dialectical materialism, that is, Difference is, of course, the very motor of a dialectic governed by a practical rather than philosophic materialism. Here, transfiguration is never complete or enduring, for the fundamental fact is poverty: to be *in*completely physical in a physical world. We call Marxism a materialism in the eighteenth-century sense in so far as matter is not, for Marx, ultimately reducible to the category of the human and its operations. However, by depositing this *essential* resistance in the realm of the mythic past, and by factoring into fully historical experience a matter which is always already transformed – a Nature which is always already culture – Marx neutralizes one idealism (absolute objects) while guarding against another (Mind). By designating as history's transformational agency class conflict (structurally, its hero: philosophically, its subject), he installs within Nature a resistance that is, for all practical purposes (and Marx entertains no others), absolute. Simply, within history, Marx's essential materialism becomes historical materialism, and since history is the history of exploitation, matter is always already *but not essentially or metaphysically* Other. The Marxian dialectic, while it dismantles the Manichean essentialisms (subject–object, mind–matter), at the same time obstructs the monism and thus the secret idealism which would seem to follow from this act. By repudiating the essential otherness of Nature and the essential identity of history, Marx deconstructs the essential subject, effectively exposing historicism's hidden agenda: its gainful reunion of the Cartesian and materialist positions. In place of that collaboration, Marx effects a prolific marriage of contraries. His historical materialism combines in a single system what would seem to be mutually exclusive concepts: absolute and historical dialectic. By this concatenation, Marx emplots an action the structural *and* dynamic principle of which is contradiction.[20]

The field of these contradictions is, as we know, the locus of change for Marx. It is the way his system avoids becoming a machine: the way history stops being, as historicism's opponents like to say, one damned thing after another. For Marx, change is the privilege-of those so objectified by the structures of the age and set so profoundly in contradiction, that their very experience of their lives constitutes a practical and *therefore* scientific critique. We recall that for historicism, like Romanticism, change is aligned with knowledge and knowledge with continuity or complementarity. The act of becoming conscious effects a change in the objective field, and a change in the direction of identity. Reduced to its subjective truth, the objective domain is smoothly assimilated or engaged by the historian. 'The music in my heart I bore / Long after it was heard no more.'

Marx's extension of Vico's discovery to the realm of Nature – his historicization of the materialist argument and its Cartesian shadow – spelt the end of historicism's dilemma. To recall in this context Coleridge's great lament, 'O Lady! we receive but what we give, / And in our life alone does Nature live', is to realize that historicism's dilemma was also the crisis of Romanticism. By that I mean the philosophic stalemate enacted for the first-generation poets by the abstract 'mind of Man and Nature' binarity, and for the second generation, by the more situated ratios of engagement vs. escape, public vs. private, England vs. elsewhere (or, following Byron, cant vs. cunt). If Nature is no essence – spirit, emptiness or objectivity – but rather mankind's ceaseless self-inscription, then the very category of Otherness, a mystery to be subjectivized or else suffered, disintegrates. This is to say, those forms of *social and historical* difference which were mystified and quarantined by the concept of the essentially alien are suddenly bound to the present by its own violence. An encounter with this order – through history, science, philosophy or literature – cannot produce a dissociated objective knowledge or an essential, subjective truth. What historicism had defined as its *antithetical* attitudes, contemplation and empathy, are revealed as a real identity and the basis of a false science. The object-knowledge engendered by the Marxian dialectic is a necessary moment in the accomplishment of an action which develops through that object and the subject who engages it. The widest and thus supplest Marxian vision allows neither the Archimedean nor the intuitive place. Similarly, it permits no victimization which will not be, in the fullness of time but not by any divinity (including Chronos), surpassed. If 'man', like Nature, is no essence, but the effect of his mode of material production, then he may, to the extent that his society enables him, change himself by changing the way he produces his life. It is my feeling – which I hope to confirm by my reading of a Wordsworth sonnet – that the perverse effectivity dramatized by the post-Revolutionary decade prevented the Romantics from inventing for themselves this crucial aspect of the Marxian argument.

In our readiness to submit the Nature and consciousness of the past to a historically objective investigation – to define the reality of the past's appearances – we have produced a strong version of the old historicism, much as Marx did. In our reluctance to reverse the dialectic, thereby yielding up our own subjectivity to a critique by the past, we have rejected that moment in the Marxian argument which would put us outside the hermeneutic circle precisely by situating us within it. The new historicism, by divorcing Marx's method from his argument, has jammed the dialectic. The motor runs but the car doesn't go because we won't operate the dialectic diachronically. By the metaphor, we refuse to put the engine in gear. This is not so perverse as it seems. By disengaging the Marxian content with its dramatically progressive narrative, we obstruct the development of a logic that would relate the contradictions of one age to the formations of another. Specifically, we construct for ourselves an experience of freedom and power with respect to our negotiations with the past. Of course we pay a price for this pleasure. Without the teleological framework, we cannot articulate our relation to the poetry we study, and without that articulation, our criticism must be but a weak version of that poetry: a repetition of its more vivid knowledge.

I'd like to demonstrate some of the general claims offered above: principally, the fact that Romanticism and historicism represent solutions to a common problem. Wordsworth's sonnet 'The world is too much with us' (Sonnet 18 in the Miscellaneous sequence, Part I, 1807 edition) brings out the effective identity of what had seemed to be distinctly antithetical positions. By its imaginative embrace of Greece's 'creed outworn' – positioned as a critical alternative to the acquisitive materialism of the age – the poem rejects the recently revitalized creed of the Roman Republic, the ruling idea of the Revolution. The double-edged allusion brings into relation one materialism – a high, philosophic kind – with another that is mean and practical. The textual superposition of these two materialisms discovers to us both the historical inscription of that abstract Romantic dualism, *Formtrieb–Stofftrieb*, and, within the historical field, the effective identity of those contraries. Ultimately, the discourse of this sonnet aligns the economic project of a particular class with the universalist philosophy of the Enlightenment. Thus are the driving interests of the Revolution brought to the surface. The poem's simple, even shallow argument locates the deep truth of Enlightenment materialism: a complement to and consequence of the Cartesian paradigm and an instrument of the class that would appropriate the prestige of that model. Wordsworth knows his subject inside out. The helpless complicity of his critique with the object of its contempt enables a real knowledge of that object: a knowledge that does not, however, set the poem or its author free.

II

'The world is too much with us'
Wordsworth: composed between 1802 and 1804;
first published 1807

> The world is too much with us; late and soon,　　　1
> Getting and spending, we lay waste our powers:
> Little we see in Nature that is ours;
> We have given our hearts away, a sordid boon!
> This Sea that bares her bosom to the moon;　　　5
> The winds that will be howling at all hours,
> And are up-gathered now like sleeping flowers;
> For this, for everything, we are out of tune;

It moves us not. – Great God! I'd rather be
A Pagan suckled in a creed outworn;   10
So might I, standing on this pleasant lea,
Have glimpses that would make me less forlorn;
Have sight of Proteus coming from the sea;
Or hear Old Triton blow his wreathèd horn.

Wordsworth's sonnet 'The world is too much with us' seems to give very little purchase to critical interest, and this could be said of nearly all the sonnets written between 1802 and 1804 and assembled in the 1807 edition. In 'Nuns fret not', the sonnet prefatory to the collection, Wordsworth implies that he is adopting a form more congenial to his political needs than to his poetical genius – a fluidly dialectical one. More to the point, the argument of Sonnet 18 is clear, unconflicted and doctrinally bland, its controlling rhetoric baldly indicative and its redemptive figures classically familiar. As a result, the curiosity of the conclusion is submerged. A poem of this kind – a jeremiad – should end with a monitory or hortatory gesture: a direct political intervention. Wordsworth concludes with a wistful, *wishful* and very private lament for the good old unrememberable days. Another way to frame this swerve – as we shall see, a complex displacement – is to remark the Romantic character of the sonnet. The Wordsworthian Jeremiah is a prophet looking backwards: predictably enough, to Nature and myth – in Walter Benjamin's phrase, Romanticism's 'two great reactive critiques'. So here we are, at the heart of the Romantic ideology, and by way of a poem as critically inert as it is familiar – canonically, a minor work.

We've already begun to activate this poem just by observing its formally disruptive, elegiac conclusion. The general plan is to search out the dynamic law of this disruption – the logic of its occurrence in this sonnet.[21] In isolating the discursive problem, we focus a doctrinal embarrassment as well. I refer to the fact that the covetous, privatized, and, fetishistic inscription of the Greek idea puts the opening commodity critique in a very strange light. Wordsworth's longing for a sight of the gods looks a good deal like a more refined version of that *Stofftrieb* mentality denounced in the opening lines. A vision of Proteus coming from the sea – a vision of a god, another culture's god, and a god possessed of a certain exchange-value in the literary market-place – seems more like an *illustration* of the complaint, 'Little we see in Nature that is ours' that a remedy.

The contradiction gets represented by the conspicuous placement of the 'have's in lines 12 and 13. These little pieces of predication, set off by their primary position in the line, their isolation from the governing subject 'I' and their logical alignment with the possessive 'ours', line 3, execute a rejection of the more regular and, one might say, unalienated grammatical form: the active construction. There, as in 'I see Proteus', the subject's own activity binds him to his perceptual object, which, by that same circuitry, returns the investment. Each term emerges as a *position*, its identity constructed by the movement of its dialectical counterpart.

We see that Wordsworth's phrase brings out the complete, and, *categorical* difference separating the 'I' from its reified glimpses and sights, and then again, dividing these sights from their material cause. Proteus, split off from the more intimate 'I'–my glimpses coupling, is syntactically fixed as the necessary condition of privileged, reflexive sensation. At the same time, the removal from the subject of its action potential – the figuring of 'I' as the passive proprietor of sensation – gives that functionary god the edge in consciousness production. The subject must wait for his meanings – glimpses and symbols – upon Nature's uncertain generosity.

Wordsworth means, of course, to frame his persona as the proper heir to a natural typology, and thus, as the owner of a consciousness redeemed from the sordid materialism of the age by the distinction of its perceptual contents as by the effortlessness of their acquisition. The sensory and cultural fetishism, however, along with the yielding of semiotic authority to a mechanically conceived first and efficient cause, the pronounced possessiveness of the discourse and the grammatical self-alienation, all conspire to *identify* the narrator with the particular corrupt sociality he deplores.

It Must Be Abstract

In order to situate this irony, we translate it into that philosophic code elaborated in the first part of this paper.[22] The detour discovers to us in the governing formal contradiction of Wordsworth's sonnet a surprising conjunction of the *cogito* with an acquisitive materialism. Lines 9–14 deliver the Cartesian salient: the reading-at-sight. The narrator yearns for the immediate cognition of a naturally symbolic world: a world that is perfectly unalienated because perfectly – aprioristically – conceptual. The desired vision of Proteus and Triton is, literally, the image of a landscape 'impressed' with 'thoughts of more deep seclusion'. It gives 'the picture of the mind' – a transhistorical, essential mind – revived again. To mark the fetish Wordsworth makes of the *cogito* and its Hellenic content is, once again, to focus his imagined antithesis to the vulgar materialism of the age as a recapitulation and also, far worse, as the very law of consciousness. The world is indeed too much with us.

The specifically *political* materialism hiding in Wordsworth's Cartesian procedures emerges in the sonnet's second logical bind. By the allusion to a 'creed outworn', the innocently indicative statement of the poem crystallizes as a negation and the whole discourse is thrown into a new register. Whatever Greece represented in the Romantic mind, it was *not* a creed. One could even say that Greece signified the *difference* between an ethos and a creed, a difference linguistically invoked by Wordsworth in his Revolutionary romance 'The Borderers'.[23] Through the word 'ethos', the age fantasized a society that, by a natural necessity and in all its domains, expresses its immanent causal law. 'Creed', by contrast, implied action mechanically derived from some doctrine or code – a causality extrinsic to its effects and, by the very fact of its *production*, informed by sectarian interests. The most spectacular recent example of this causal principle was, plainly, the late-phase French Revolution. One might even infer that the extended Revolutionary era instanced in the contemporary British mind the metamorphosis of an expressive, organic causality into a mechanical mode of determination; hence the grotesque discrepancy between causes and effects. Or, whatever it was *France* came to represent, it was *also* a creed.

The wrongheadedness of Wordsworth's name for the Greek idea arises from its double-duty in the poem. The phrase is enjoined to repudiate a creed *forsworn* and, I'll argue, the very notion of creedal action. The line in question, translated into its authentic form, would read: 'Great god, I'd rather *not* be a rational creature, suckled in that "pernicious philosophism" spawned by the Enlightenment.' 'Pagan', here, means not just Greek, but anti-Roman, and Roman means suckled by that she-wolf, philosophy.[24] The violent attack upon a selfishly calculating mentality is also a critique of what had looked like a nobly calculating spirit: eighteenth-century rationalism. Hence, perhaps, the fervour of the opening diatribe. What Wordsworth hates, he also loved, or loves.

Finally, the abrupt shift from the 'we' of the octet to the 'I' of the sestet – in conjunction with the longing for prestigious sensations and the covert reference to the Enlightenment creed – outlines *within the idealist paradigm* the shadow of that high, philosophic materialism. The invective against a crass commercialism (lines 2–4), and the hedonistic critique of a pragmatic rationalism (5–8), are both carried out by a Cartesian strategy: regression to the contemplative stance. By conferring this noble look upon a longing he has already disfigured, Wordsworth inscribes both materialisms – the vulgar and highminded – within the dominion of the *cogito*, deconstructing, in effect, the age's binary political positions: Revolution and reaction, lower and upper. Only one form could emerge from that Manichean wreckage: business and the bourgeoisie, the middle terms.

In order to learn *why* Wordsworth's poem so cruelly betrays itself, we move out towards a textual and compositional context. In both the 1807 and 1815 editions, Wordsworth places Sonnet 18 (#33, 1815) under the Miscellaneous rubric, segregating it from the openly political sonnets, those Dedicated to (National Independence and) Liberty. Nearly all the sonnets are products of the period 1802–4 – loosely, the period between two wars and strictly, the interval separating the two movements of the Intimations Ode. Wordsworth wrote stanzas 1–4 of the Ode in March 1802, on the very day that concluded the negotiations for the Peace of Amiens. The fourth stanza of the Ode closes upon these familiar lines: 'Whither is fled the visionary gleam? / Where is it now, the glory and the dream?' In an essay on the Ode, I put this question in the field of contemporary politics and with reference to the dispiriting final proof that the gloriously collective dream – the vision – of Wordsworth's young manhood had been but a shared hallucination. Wordsworth resumed the Ode in 1804. The famous Neoplatonic myth of the soul is his attempt to contextualize his loss (figured as a private, and abstractly existential tragedy), in a metaphysical terrain, where he could give it the look of a tolerably fortunate fall.

Obviously, neither the sonnet nor the Ode is a sustained allegory of the Revolutionary era. But like the Ode, the sonnet imagines by its style a mythic explanation of the awful logic of that age. Both poems develop as answers to that unanswerable question, 'whither is fled the visionary gleam'. The Ode speaks from the position of loss and despair. The project of the sonnet is denial. Wordsworth knows where that hopeful energy went; it is change, not loss which is found so unbearable in this poem.

It Must Change

Now that we've set the poem – loosely, to be sure – in this more immediate political field, we can start reading it in the mode of 'structural difference and determinate contradiction'.[25] What had looked like a continuous, accretive argument breaks up into three dynamically related sections. In the opening quatrain, we detect some complicity between the form of Wordsworth's critique and its object. The abstract statement – utterance of a placeless moral sage – reminds us of the philosophic voices of the late eighteenth century. Moreover, the conduct of the argument – proof by isolation of the rational principle governing material phenomena – conforms to that method we call analytic reason, a method strongly associated with the Enlightenment programme.

To see this is also to observe that the following passage sketches by its propositional form a twofold critique of the opening statement.

> This Sea that bares her bosom to the moon;
> The winds that will be howling at all hours,
> And are up-gathered now like sleeping flowers;
> For this, for everything, we are out of tune;

In their *structural* relation to the first movement, lines 5–7 instance a dialectical rather than analytic logic. We see too that the form of the utterance is demonstrative – not, as in lines 1–4, predicative. As we read on, however, we find that the wonderfully immanent phrases are prepositional appositions. The penultimate clause – 'For this, for everything, we are out of tune' – restores that analytically abstractive law which governs the opening lines.

The formal critique is thus compromised; one has to conclude that the effective work of the section is performed by its content. Both images, Sea and winds, graph a particular action mode, determined by a moment of primary generosity. The figures install between – or rather, beyond – 'getting and spending' the special gestural mode of 'giving'. This is, of course, a recompensed or dialectical generosity. The Sea that gives to the moon her beautiful image is, in the selfsame moment, adorned by its answering light. As for the winds, the simile whereby Wordsworth expresses their dynamic poise ('like sleeping flowers'), sketches a grateful vicissitude of matter and form, substance and energy. In the poem, this organic generosity represents a high hedonism, the direct antithesis of both the low and high rationalisms Wordsworth is keen to discredit. The critique is of calculation in any form.

The final section formulates the image logic of the preceding quatrain by reference to that near-topos of beauty, freedom and power: Greece. Here, we might say, is Schiller's solution to the contrary *Form* and *Stoff* impulses, both of them registered in the opening lines and figurally opposed by the *Spieltrieb* dynamic of the middle section. Moreover, by the Miltonic allusion, line 13, Wordsworth associates this figure with the philosopher's stone. He would seem to have solved the problem of the analytic intellect in the happiest way.[26]

One must feel, however, in the markedly passive phrasing of the last few lines, a backing off from the organic dialectic graphed in the middle section. Lines 9–14 execute a withdrawal from the wilfulness of action itself, independent of any particular agency, and also a retreat from a kinetic, reciprocally transformative concept of subjectivity. The work of the conclusion is to surpass the moment of primary generosity (Sea and winds), by a swerve towards the recipient position: the spectator, the listener. Wordsworth *more* than undoes the dialectically braided action of lines 5–7; he indicates that the genuine critique of a getting–spending economy is not an action form at all (say, *Spieltrieb*), but instead, a form of possession, in both senses of that word. In the poem, *giving* opposes *getting* (*spending*'s content), and is itself displaced by *receiving*, the better antithesis to *getting* and the transcendence of expense. The content of the fantasy is Hellenic but, by this passional, paradoxical emphasis, we discern a correctively Christian form. The desire for vision is a desire for revelation: not the experience of a world evenly instinct with meaning (the classical, or Pagan world), but the disclosure of a world distinguished by Meaning, the Christian world. Wordsworth solicits the vision of the gods as 'a leading from above, a something given'.

We can say, then, that the third quatrain hollows out the analytic critique of the first and the figural critique of the second by proposing the deficiency of the very notion of critique. The assertive critical gesture of Part 3 is, *precisely*, escape. Through his retreat to the past – an abandonment of both culture (Part 1) and Nature (Part 2) – the narrator learns that culture and Nature are one and they wear the human face divine.

A close study of this face shows the method of the retreat. Wordsworth translates the natural imagery of lines 5–7 – a sublime iconography that had served the Revolution as one of its privileged discourses – into the beautiful images of the Greek pantheon. Proteus coming from the Sea *is* the Sea of line 5, in a finer tone, just as Triton blowing his horn *is* the redemptive wind, line 6. In this context, supernatural naturalism would seem to be the appropriate phrase, with the supernatural taking the form of a prestigious cultural product – one that, by the grammar of contemporary iconographies, disavowed another such product, the Roman idea. By this trick of translation, Wordsworth secures his special vantage on contemporary life, the condition of his special form of social criticism. The reader who consents to this Archimedean place must also reject the analytic and figural critiques, lines 1–9: or, the unfreedom of both the satiric-prophetic and the apocalyptically corrective methods. One is meant to see that the authentic criticism is renunciation of criticism; the solution to the problem is dissolution of the problematic; the remedial thought is that queer, contentless thought that lies too deep for tears. In 'less forlorn', we are meant to feel and approve the narrator's rejection of the organic hedonism of lines 5–8 – an expressive causality – and, of the mechanical principles coded in the opening lines, as in the guiding doctrines of the Revolution. Wordsworth leaves behind action and desire and he asks us, by way of far better compensation, to endorse as the properly political discourse what we might call 'aesthetic scholarship', a phrase that has been used to characterize a dominant form of historicism.[27]

What I've done so far is to outline the sonnet's way of relating

'Wordsworth' to 'anti-Wordsworth', individual life to an inimically conceived social domain. What remains is to move beyond that social outside to which the poem refers by suppression, negation and distortion, to some more compelling order of meaning, one that is unimagined – unimaginable – by Wordsworth's text.[28]

Apropos Wordsworth's subjunctive mood – its normative role in the poem – we recall that an essentialist materialism, because it cannot know its own knowledge without reinstating a mind–matter distinction, effectively defines self-consciousness as sheer negativity, exactly the metaphysical presence its doctrine denies. We are left with the purest Cartesian figure: the subject as connoisseur of his own, categorically estranged consciousness. This is a model of mind distinguished by the incommensurability of its content and form, its 'for' and 'in' itself. We have seen that Wordsworth's sonnet figures consciousness as both an object for possession ('so might I / Have') and a social representation: sign of professional access and elevation, of 'culture'. Further, the poem identifies this second-nature by disjunction and emptiness: in the text's affective language, rejection and desire. Even as we glimpse in this psychic projection an idealizing picture of the commodity form – that supple confusion, the possession of which famishes the craving – we see that in the context of the awesome Revolutionary dialectic, its negativity represents a keen insight. It signifies that neither knowledge nor practice offers escape from the body politic: that no position is not also its contrary. All that we have in Nature that is ours, then, is our refusal and desire, a negativity that, as such, cannot be complicit with the world, which is nothing if not presence.

This is the grim wisdom Wordsworth salvages from his despair. But again, the verbal form of this wisdom – the poem's abstractive fetishism – betrays the deep antagonism of even our own desire, proving that our negations of the given are always already compromised.

We begin, I think, to grasp the viciously redundant energy of this sonnet, and to understand the plangent tone of the sestet. Not only does the form of inwardness developed in that section reproduce the hated commodity form of the octet, but the concept of the self as an owner, constituted by its necessarily alienated property (its sights, for example), reproduces the dynamic of the general, constituted by his conquests, the emperor, realized by his subjects. If 'I' am, essentially, my own property – a quality I engender by my (negative) encounters with the physical world – then, in order simply to endure, I must ceaselessly remake myself in my own image. In the language of Enlightenment libertarianism, I must tirelessly exercise my rights in order to deserve them. If I refuse this responsibility, I cease to be fully human and therefore cease to be a natural claimant to these rights. A mind that is not constantly self-estranging – reproducing itself by re-alienating its stock of consciousness – is a mind constantly self-consuming.

Then too, a self conceived as self-possession has *value* only as a representation, for what is the meaning of privileged possession outside a community of other, differentially defined owners? To name myself the owner of my mind is to make myself the owner of a sign that indicates rather than instances my worth. Even as I designate my value, then, I mystify it. The mystery, or the prestige that attends it, has its price, well known to those of us conversant with the anxieties of the Romantic self. By defining myself as the owner of my mind – something I experience only to the extent that it is 'not me' and that has value only in so far as I alienate it yet again by representing it – I make myself that strictly negative thing which is *not* that which I own and *not* the signs by which I designate that ownership. Similarly, all that I own – my consciousness as content or object – must be maintained as 'not me'. It must be kept not just unassimilated, but (here's the complete paradox) *unrightful* property.

I trace this circle for three reasons. First, it gives a richer, tougher context to the epistemological anguishing and psychic dissonance that distinguish the Romantic repertoire. Second, it foregrounds the special problems arising for a writer who conceived his literary exercise as a critique of the rising class (first from the left, then the right), a writer compelled by history to observe in the very form of that critique the logic of both the Napoleonic and the bourgeois projects. Third, our circle brings into relation a form of consciousness and a form of material production. The freedom to own one's consciousness and to valorize oneself by that property is also the freedom of the worker to own, to price and to sell his labour. The later part of the century discovered the monstrous bondage of this kind of freedom. Here again we gloss the forlornness of the sestet and see that it is the by-product, not the impetus, of Wordsworth's return to his sole self. At the same time, we see that the discourse of this poem, by figuring the bourgeois truth of the Revolution and the exploitation at the heart of that truth, strikes out beyond 1807. It anticipates this reading.

Wordsworth's inability to antithesize his thesis engenders the structural binds I've marked off. We can now work those contradictions as a mode of relation. What concerns me here is the Miltonic allusion Wordsworth develops in this, as in so many of the 1807 sonnets. The voice of lines 1–4 is that strong, scolding voice one associates so specifically with Milton, or with Milton in his forward-looking phase. This voice seems sharply inconsistent with the plaintive notes of the sestet until we remember Milton's own changes – like Wordsworth's, the result of deep political disappointments. Yet again, then, and by way of Milton's great cause, Wordsworth's sonnet entertains the Revolution. In the tonal hiatus between octet and sestet, we glimpse that disappointment, just as the Puritan Revolution mediates Milton's angry and inward phases.

The analogy teaches us something about the failure of both Revolutions. The hectoring octet is connected to the dreamy sestet by the isolation of both voices, Puritan and Jacobin, from their constituencies. The prophets looking forwards and back each *represent* their social orders, and they draw their power from the distance and negativity of that posture. The loneliness of Wordsworth's (and Milton's) post-Revolutionary voice is only a form of that strong, self-imposed isolation that energizes the early poetry. Wordsworth *knows* what it is that binds him to Milton: 'Thy soul was like a Star, and dwelt apart.' Ironically, Wordsworth's rhetorical stance – that of what Stevens calls the 'major man' – recapitulates the dynamic he properly condemns: the idea of a creed or doctrine, the reified interest of a distinct group, *representing* a general way of life. In this sonnet, Wordsworth produces the knowledge that change initiated by an essentially conceived subject – irrespective of its representational generosity – necessarily means change in the interest of a particular group and thus against the common good. Because Wordsworth does not, however, recognize this knowledge, the sonnet vibrates with a patriarchal force. Until Pound's angry Cantos, we do not hear again the resonance of these 1807 sonnets.

Even as we cite the sonnet's failure to name its knowledge, we observe that the extremity of its contradictions forces out an alternative to its agonistic solution. Neither an ethos nor a creed, neither Greece nor France; not an expressive and not a mechanical causality. We begin to imagine a group that lives in full awareness a consciousness produced by its ongoing life activity. We derive from this fantasy an idea of social action which would express and engender, if not identical, then transitively organized subject/object forms. Here, in *our* fantasy, is the political unconscious of Wordsworth's sonnet. Here too is the anti-Enlightened theme of the 'Ode to Duty': its wish, 'to do thy will and know it not'. Finally, here is the authentic Greek meaning, come to displace the fetishized mythos of Wordsworth's sonnet.

We have seen how that meaning turns, in and upon Wordsworth's fallen text: how the utopian desire takes on the body of the age. From Wordsworth's pronounced rhetorical retreat (from the social 'we', from the present, from the indicative to the subjunctive, analysis to reverie), as from his selection of the confining sonnet form, we infer the explicit longing of the poem. The sonnet dreams of a world where partial consciousness, regarded as the necessary condition *of* consciousness, is so constant in its operation that it seamlessly adapts us to – better yet, displaces – the order of things.[29] This is, we know, a definition of ideology, and of ideology as world duplication.[30] The complaint of the poem might thus be rewritten, 'the world is too much *with* us: not enough *in* us, *of* us.' The desire for the gods is the wish of a man who has felt the weight of too much liberty, of Reason in its several moods. We recall Wordsworth's famous, early disclaimer of 'distinct purpose formally conceived', we remember how his deeply cathected purposes returned in nightmare form to torment him, and we realize that the longing of this sonnet, as of so many Romantic poems, is to be shut of Reason and its purposes altogether.[31]

Wordsworth's solution to the consciousness problem of his age – his imagination of alternative modes of possession: an imagination 'transcending' the invention of alternative action modes – is, then, both a defence and, beyond the horizon of Wordsworth's knowledge, an offensive, a class move. The very concreteness of Wordsworth's solution, as well as its manifest failure, puts us on the other side of Wordsworth's horizon: in a position to see it, that is. By this poem, we learn that consciousness must redeem itself through changes in the mode of production, not possession. We can say at this point that the contradictions of Wordsworth's sonnet, which I take as epochally symptomatic, do not anticipate the Marxian solution, they precipitate it.

The Romantic gravity of this poem is not, naturally, a thematic affair. We find anti-materialist invectives in Ben Jonson, Pope and Swift. What makes Wordsworth's poem so powerfully Romantic a discourse – and this despite its Horatian *hauteur* and its Miltonic harangue – is the way it produces and projects its critique.

We have seen Wordsworth expose the corrupt social reality of his time from the standpoint of Nature and myth. We have also seen that this corrupt sociality is just what constitutes Nature and myth symbolic and also critical alternatives for the poets of the early nineteenth century. What makes this sonnet so Romantic, then, is the incompleteness of its dialectical plot: as if the critically objectifying act does not also and always falsify the masterful subject it brings into being. Wordsworth can represent, albeit by displacement, the historical and even economic premises of the French Revolution and its Roman costume, but he cannot *conceive* his particular Greek and organic ideas.

These concepts are, in effect, set aside. The gesture is an attempt to protect a certain subject-position, gravely jeopardized in the field of contemporary practice, as we've seen. Wordsworth's Greece – Nature and myth in one bundle – marks out the transformative spot, the visionary dell of this poem. The idea of Nature as a critical escape from culture rather than its product and servant, and of the past as a prospect on the present and not its absent cause, includes the idea that the cultivated person can engage his moment by knowledge, sensation or reverie – can engage it, that is, by escaping it. For those three words, in the context of the early 1800s, were a way of describing and maintaining a safety zone separating causes from their baleful effects, mind from the matter it had set in motion, politics from a poetry that faced the impossible task of continuing to imagine itself a first and a final cause and at the same time innocent. As we know, the ideas behind those three words, 'knowledge', 'sensation', 'reverie', underwrote a mode of production that divorced material from mental labour, existence from consciousness, life from art. Or, ideology arises in order to mediate what certain modes of production continuously put asunder. By ideology, I mean, once again, the illusion of a selectively dialectical knowledge. Romantic poetry figures this critical command in its many resorts, retreats and elevations: positive figures for both the suffered *and the desired* divisions. In these sad lines from Wordsworth's Ode, 'My heart is at your festival, / My head hath its coronal, / The fulness of your bliss, I feel – I feel it all,' *we* feel both the insight of the heart/head distinction, and, in the limpness of the protest, the cherished lie. Similarly, even as we sense in the sonnet something more than regret for the lost, lapsed communality of the Greek world, Wordsworth's insistence on the privacy of this sentiment and of the insight it expresses marks the poem as a completely Romantic work: torn apart by its helpless intelligence.

There is a final and a happier phase to this critique, and it proceeds by way of some trivial material. I refer to those very unWordsworthian inversions, 'outworn' and 'up-gathered'. Installed within the field developed here, these words instance a categorical break. In making the effect (up, out) precede its cause (gathered, worn), these participials suggest the idea of directed, effectual action proceeding without the agency of a purposeful (in the Revolutionary context, culpable) subject. Even as we recognize the historically determined function of this figure for an innocent effectivity, we appreciate its futuristic edge. Here is the movement beyond both the mechanical causality of the first four lines and the expressive, organic mode dramatized in the rest of the octet.[32] These little words, which reject the standard linguistic movement from subject to predicate, cause to effect, sketch a movement whereby a subject is constituted as such by its action. It is only a cause, thus, after the fact and to the extent that it is also an effect. I cannot imagine a more concise verbal demonstration of the Marxian logic of consciousness, the effect of its own mode of production.

The verb form gives rise to a more global and, for us, a more serviceable reading too. Wordsworth's new usages (suggestively, a veritable idiom among the later Romantics) enable us to conceive the subject – here, Wordsworth's present – as an absent cause that exists by and in its effects, which are related to that cause by distance and difference. Wordsworth, as the full Romantic subject presented here, exists *only* here, in the detached effect of that subjectivity. By this Romantic*ist* rewriting – a decidedly literal translation of Wordsworth's own opportunistic translation from the Greek – we conjure the aura of this criticism's absent cause. I refer to that Wordsworthian Real which, though it resists symbolization absolutely, emerges in the form of that past's future: this uniquely interested reproduction. This translation of mine judges me (both individually and as an agent of my class, sex, profession and era) as Wordsworth's translation of the Greeks judges him. His poem – a richly dialectical critique – half creates and wholly condemns the practical limits of this reading. In effectuating *our* absent cause, Wordsworth's sonnet, we violate and displace it, and at the same time produce it as an absolute origin: a first and irreducible cause. What I'm proposing is the inseparability of the constitutive and deconstructive (in Sartre's phrase, progressive and regressive) moments in this process. By totalizing Wordsworth's compromise solution, we make it compromise *us*. As we know from the lesson – the object lesson – of Wordsworth's poem, the other and worse option is reification.[33]

Wordsworth's backward-looking prophet shows us the intelligence and the special dangers of that way of constructing a future: that aesthetic scholarship, that historicism. In his helplessly elegiac and, thus, self-serving critique, we recognize the very form of our literary criticism, which redeems to murder. The *reflected* production of conjunctures like these is, I believe, the sort of thing a new historicism should attempt.

III

I want to suggest very briefly a few applications of the reading I've just unfolded. You'll remember that I put the Romantic salient of Wordsworth's sonnet in its subjectively weighted and also armoured dialectic. Wordsworth's refusal to let his action upon the past rearrange his present – indeed, his denial that his looking and figuring *constitute* an action – locates for us the common factor in much of what goes by the name 'new historicism' in Romantic studies. It is this that makes our new histories so very old a tale in the chronicles of intellectual history. Among the effects of this short-circuiting are first, the inadequacy of the new historicist concept of ideology. To imagine ideology as a set of ideas and attitudes that are pre-conscious but theoretically available to the ideological subject, contemporary or belated, and available in strictly conceptual form, is to reject a dynamic concept of culture and of the unconscious. It hardly needs saying that thus do we put the idea of transparency – a place beyond ideology – *within* this fallen world, and, within the consciousness of remarkable men and women. In the end, this is to put utopia in our universities.

Second, our criticism is preoccupied with questions of blame and defence. Few of us know what to do with the contradictions we've grown so deft at exposing, discrepancies between discourse and argument, practice and profession. Because we lack, in the private sector, a dynamic notion of ideology (or, a real understanding of hegemony), and in the public sphere, a fully historical – which is to say, *trans*historical – notion of causality, we're forced to interpret these textual binds as ethical matters. I don't think even *we* are interested in our collections of literary saints and sinners. Besides, our job is not to decide whether to be charitable or severe to Wordsworth but rather to ascertain as best we can the necessity of his solutions. This is not, as it might seem, a question of tolerance or of humility: something along the lines of 'I am human therefore nothing human is alien to me.' We are in this business to keep ourselves from dreaming. A past that is continuous with the present rather than *related* to it cannot arouse us. More important, judgements of Wordsworth's political correctness and moral fibre – did he sell out, did he stand firm – establish him as a free agent: a non-ideological subject in an ideologized world. Presumably, we construct Wordsworth in this way in order to imply our comparable freedom. Apologetics for or against Wordsworth are always apologetics for us.

Third, without an attempt to reverse the critical vector, our tortuous rewritings remain abstract. Our reluctance to engage the dialectic within the present (not unlike our habit of collapsing text into context and literature into politics), is a way of reducing past and present to a single, homogeneous and historically innocent temporality. This is a sure way to empty the past of its reality and the present of its responsibility.

How then *should* we position ourselves towards the literatures of the past? How to avoid historicism's Hobson's choice of contemplation or empathy, a discourse of knowledge or of power? One might propose that in a real and practical way, *we are the effects* of particular pasts, to which we are related by distance and difference. Those pasts could be bound to us as the absent cause is linked to the effects which embody it. To say this is to identify that second and difficult Real of which Althusser writes – not the binary opposite to the age's Imaginary but that which resists symbolization absolutely – with the future, some *particular* future. By our ideological practice, we produce Wordsworth's absolute Real and in so doing, we catapult *our* Real to some unimaginable point in the future. We do this with a certain panache; we *send* the content of our criticism beyond its phrase. We *invite* the generations that succeed us to tread us down: totalize our phrases and violate our knowledge. If this violence presses out *our* Real in symbolic form, then we will have anticipated the future and there *will have been* a meaning to that which we suffer in our lives because we cannot conceive it. This is an ironic view of history as lived and a comic view of history as reproduced by the future. It is, following Benjamin, the gift of the destructive character.

How do we know which past we are in position to realize; which past is ready to begin its posthumous life now? This is a question that can only be answered in a practical and circular way. One asks oneself which periods are generating the most interest and producing the most interesting criticism. Which group of critics seems most passionate, most defensive and extreme? Which is the most awkward in its rhetoric and difficult in its forms of argumentation? Which discourse sounds the most theological? Exciting work is always being done across the board; one needs to find out which group of historians feels most vividly a sense of mission and of solidarity.

We know there are moments when two ages call to each other in powerful ways. Naturally, there are strong local reasons – institutional reasons – for these conjunctions. But we must also wonder if there aren't other orders of explanation. Might we not be part of a developing, leap-frogging logic? Are we, or could we *make* ourselves the consciousness of the Romantic movement produced as a moment in the accomplishment of that action? To ask this is to wonder who we are that we produce the Romantics in just this way. It is also to inquire who *they* are, to have produced *us* in just this way. Once again, we go *back* to the future.

To ask these questions is to insist that we rewrite the past with the full complement of contemporary knowledges. It is also to name ourselves as producers of the past *as past* and thus of history's meaning, even as we bring out the historical overdetermination of our productive acts and even as we renounce a fully dialectical knowledge of ourselves. We define ourselves as a potential structure to be actualized by whatever generation it is that turns around and seeks us out as its way of living its present. This model is, among other things, a way to establish the absolute difference between past and present but also to see that this difference is a form of complicity.

For the old historicism, the alleged project was to restore to the dead their own, living language, that they might bespeak themselves. Historicism defined, as we know, a sort of ventriloquism – a virtuoso variety. The dummy really seems to speak; the ventriloquist does not move his lips.

By contrast, the critical work I've been describing should be called translation. One of the phrases that recurs throughout today's criticism is 'rewriting the past'. We refresh the cliché by way of Benjamin's great essay, 'The Task of the Translator'. The formal analogy gains a certain force from Benjamin's own sense of its relevance to our Romantic concerns.

> It is no mere coincidence that the word 'ironic' [apropos the relation of translation to original] brings the Romanticists to mind; they more than any others were gifted with an insight into the life of literary works which has its highest testimony in translation. To be sure, they hardly recognized translation in this sense, but devoted their entire attention to criticism, another, if a lesser factor in the continued life of literary works.[34]

Benjamin asks a shocking question: 'is translation meant for readers who do not understand the original?' He goes on, 'for what does a literary work say. It tells very little to those who understand it.' There is, naturally, a conventional – indeed, a Romantic – way of reading the remark. I paraphrase: 'Great literature, as all good readers know, has no content. It has transmuted all that raw facticity into soul and form.' There is also, however, the strong reading: literature tells very little to those whose ideology reproduces it, who can represent it to themselves, conceive it – in short, understand it. Such readers can be 'edified' by the work (and we recall Benjamin's scorn for edification). They can, that is, be 'built up, improved' (the root meaning of 'edify'). They cannot, however, be taken apart, and this is what art, for most of us, seems to be about. The translation, then, is meant for those who come at some *particular* 'later', one that compels them to produce their lives in a way not just different from but antagonistic to the way of the original. Because of this, they cannot read the original properly. Therefore they can put it to work.

To put this practically, we could say that all works become avant-garde at a particular point in time which is the beginning of their posthumous existence. The job of the translator-critic – our job – is to produce this point of departure. We can only do this by producing a bad, a literal, translation, one that, by misunderstanding the spirit of the original, *represents* the work's resistance to those who 'do not speak its tongue', who do not share, that is, its ideology. Translation of this kind pronounces the original's ineffability yet preserves its silence. It demonstrates the original's strong difference from the present age, and, at the same time, shows that only this age, these barbarians, can change the work and be changed by it. This parodic translation is, then, the exemplary act of literary appreciation since it is the only repetition that leaves the original intact. It is also the most invasive kind of criticism imaginable. Or, to rewrite Benjamin's question, and as an answer, *originals* are meant for those who do not understand them; they are meant for the criticism of the future.

This is the real power of art-works – not just to survive (the classic 'classic' definition) but to flare up at a certain moment, thereby introducing their distinct order of production into the alien formations of another age. One is reminded of that trusty translation metaphor, 'old wine in new bottles'. The phrase is a good one so long as it is taken to signify the *contradiction* between old and new. It is this friction that realizes the old, and that gives the new – the critique or translation – *its* power to flare up later. Only by the differential of another intention can the intention of those first words crystallize. This sort of dialogism is exactly the aim of that critical ravishing, that literalism, I have described.[35]

In order to use what is thrust upon us – Romantic poetry or its academic form, historicism – our criticism must first be abstract: a repetition detoured through the concepts of the present. It must change: meaning, it must change the past, and let itself *be changed* by its own invention. Finally, it must give pleasure. Thus do we prescribe that 'libidinal investment' Jameson has discussed. We ask of our criticism a susceptibility to reduction, such that the present can use it for its own exercises in the imaginary. We do all this because the literatures of the past, if left to themselves, confront us as despotic structures: what Sartre calls totalities as opposed to totalizations. The more resonant phrase is 'practico-inert'. It's not a question, as historicism thought, of calling up the past and making it speak. The past is with us all the time and it never stops speaking. Without an aggressive re-enactment of the past, it re-enacts us. One thinks of that nightmare of familiarity — that terrible, because imperial, family romance, 'The Shining'. One thinks of those importunate ghosts and feels the hideousness of the past when it gets *passively* re-enacted.

Benjamin tells us 'it is not the highest praise of a translation to say that it reads as if it had been written in that language.' This business of re-totalizing is a corrosive affair. Benjamin advises a 'literal rendering of the syntax which proves words rather than sentences to be the primary element of the translator'. We have seen in our reading of Wordsworth's sonnet how material a rewriting of the past this protocol entails. Benjamin finds at the end of this process a 'pure language, which no longer means or expresses anything but is as the expressionless and creative Word, that which is meant in all languages'. To take the mystical edge off this and to coordinate it with some earlier remarks, we may identify this Word with the Real which resists symbolization absolutely and which is therefore experienced as necessity. By our criticism, we configurate our own, unimaginable Real with the Real of 1802, and while we cannot *remember* that Real — cannot, therefore, teach it — we can, by our bad repetition, represent it. The effect one hopes to produce by one's criticism is that of shock: deep familiarity and profound difference. It took 150 years to hear 'The world is too much with us, late and soon' with a certain ring. This is definitely *not* the ring heard by Wordsworth's contemporaries. One hopes it is a ring different enough from all those sounds and some of our own, and in the right ways, for it to make Wordsworth's phrase re-sound, to make it 'tell', in Benjamin's sense, which is the opposite of 'teach'.

Up until now, Romantic poetry was not categorically different from the literary output of any other age. Because it lacked a distinctive kind of pastness, it had no distinctive presentness either. To read Romantic poetry tendentiously – for ourselves – we effectively read it by its own latest dream. In the selfsame motion and by feeling the lateness of our dream, we alter our own language. 'The basic error of the translator is that he preserves the state in which his own language happens to be rather than allowing his language to be affected by the foreign tongue.' The translator-critic does not redeem the past, he – or she – conceives it, by an action that might remind us of Yeats's 'Leda and the Swan', an action that produced Helen, Troy, Homer and history. We do *to* the past what it could not do *for* itself. We see it clearly in the idea of it.

Notes

1 This model of knowledge derives from Georg Lukács' postulate of the proletariat as capitalism's working self-consciousness and thus as the internal surpassing of the special epistemological bind required by that economic order. 'Reification and the Consciousness of the Proletariat', in *History and Class Consciousness*, trans. Rodney Livingstone (Cambridge, Mass.: MIT Press, 1971), pp. 83–222.
2 These four orders are our resistance to Yale, our revisionary interest in historical scholarship, the historiographic forms of the nineteenth century, and the Marxian methodology.
3 (1) Alan Bewell, David Bromwich, Jim Chandler, Jerome Christensen, Kurt Heinzelman, Kenneth Johnston, Anne Mellor, Cliff Siskin, Olivia Smith; (2) John Barrell, Marilyn Butler, Laurence Goldstein, Paul Hamilton, Alan Liu, Jerry McGann, Marjorie Levinson, David Simpson. The two groupings represent a discrimination along methodological and political lines.
4 We inscribe our reaction to the historical studies of the past fifty years in our multiply pregnant self-designation. By the locution 'new historicism' – with its resonance to the 'new criticism' and its grammatical rejection of the subordinate adjectival form 'historical' – we pronounce the critical invasiveness of our scholarly procedures. We dissolve the intrinsic–extrinsic distinctions felt to govern the old, historical scholarship so as to move beyond the peripheral, illustrative character of that exercise.

Our rejection of Yale's present-mindedness is a more complicated matter. One might even glimpse in the reactive empiricism which regularly surfaces in today's criticism an idealism not all that different from Yale's more manifestly tendentious abstractness. I refer to the way in which 'politics' or 'history' gets *practically* identified with that otherwise abandoned domain: the absolute, irreducible, matter-of-fact. To install a Real in this binary fashion is of course to construct another ghost town, and one a good deal more dangerous than New Haven, as its ghosts are so much more lifelike. Moreover, our tendency to homogenize text and context by collapsing them all into the category 'social text' – a consequence of our semiotic sophistication – consorts very strangely with our postulate of a Real which is some kind of final intransigence. In short, we seem oddly reluctant to think dialectically. Either we reduce text and context to 'social text' – mediations both, their authority intertextual, not extrinsic – or we elevate literature and life to the status of self-authorizing immediacies.

5 Today's historicism is a historically informed investigation of the representational acts that made and make both literary objects and their receptions. The idea is to situate politics within the work and, typically, at the level of its allusive structure. Literary mode of production (roughly, form), and ideology as it operates to realize this given productive mode in particular ways for particular writers (roughly, style), do not have an important place in this criticism. Historicists tend to focus on representational objects as these figure by displacement, absence or distortion in the work. When they *do* reflect on the verbal surface as such, they generally treat it as a mimetic dimension as well: a reference to some extraliterary occurrence of a particular linguistic item. Or, style is read as an authorial selection of a particular political code, its partisanship clearly established within the domain of contemporary culture.

By 'politics', historicists seem to intend actual circumstances and their apparent interrelations, as well as the covert logic obtaining among these data in the contemporary mind. Rarely are these configurations set within a larger, and in some way compelling objective field. In note 4, I observe a tendency in our criticism to synonymize 'politics' with the Real of the poet's time and place. The manner in which the work figures (disfigures, deconstructs or dismisses), this referential order indicates both the work's ideological position and the conflicts pertaining to that place. 'Position' tends to be treated as a static phenomenon rather than a dynamic, problem-solving function. Historicists do not, that is, generally assume the ongoing proliferation of positions by a contradiction-engendering base of any kind. As for 'ideology', this appears to mean something like involuntary insertion in a cultural force field. This insertion carries with it or is constituted by a set of attitudes and beliefs not easily accessible to consciousness but theoretically available to the ideological subject.

Those who produce the new historicism are trying to respond to the so-called failure of empiricism less antithetically than the scholarship of this century reacted to the hegemony of the new criticism. Now that the poststructuralisms have demonstrated the absolutely mediated form in which history is lived and remembered – the narrativity of historical knowledge and experience – we fold text and context into a variegated but homogeneous batter. Rather than tell stories, in the sense of genetic narrations or accounts of developing projects, historicists favour a cross-referencing mode of analysis, wherein the mechanical relations of social to literary text are traced in both directions. This preference for marble cakes over layer cakes would seem to betray a wish to live that 'molarity' we image. In lieu of this Imaginary solution, a collapse of the text–context distinction as this got formulated in particular works and periods, we might *develop* that difference and then *relate* it to the contradiction between our own everyday life and our professional consciousness. We might use our *own* longing in order to illuminate the continuity dreams of the works we study; by that practice, we begin to refocus, maybe even to alter the form of our wishes.

6 Tony Bennett, *Formalism and Marxism* (London: Methuen, 1979), pp. 167, 168.
7 Jean-Paul Sartre, *Search for a Method*, trans. Hazel Barnes (New York: Random House, 1968; rpt. 1963), p. 99 note 4.
8 Sartre, *Search for a Method*, p. 33 note 9.
9 This construct represents a crossing of Althusser's concept, structural causality, and Sartre's discussion of totalization. See Louis Althusser and Etienne Balibar, *Reading Capital*, trans. Ben Brewster (London: New Left Books, 1970), pp. 184–93; Sartre, *Search for a Method*, pp. 133–66; and *Critique of Dialectical Reason*, trans. Alan Sheridan-Smith, ed. Jonathan Ree (London: New Left Books, 1982), pp. 53–252. I am indebted to Fredric Jameson's own implicit alignment of these positions, *The Political Unconscious* (Ithaca, NY: Cornell University Press, 1981), pp. 33–58, 74–102.
10 This notion of a history running in two directions at once, the progressive movement actually reconstituting the past, thereby changing the present (the point of departure) and future as well, is my version of Sartre's 'progressive–regressive method', elaborated in his *Search for a Method*.
11 Wesley Morris, *Toward a New Historicism* (Princeton, NJ: Princeton University Press, 1972), pp. 3–13; Hans Meyerhoff, (ed.), *The Philosophy of History in our Time* (New York: Doubleday, 1959); J. C. D. Clark, *English Society: 1688–1832* (Cambridge: Cambridge University Press, 1985).
12 Fredric Jameson, *The Political Unconscious* (Ithaca, NY: Cornell University Press, 1981), p. 29. This whole argument derives more than I can estimate from Jameson's 'Marxism and Historicism', *New Literary History*, vol. 11, no. 1 (Autumn 1979), pp. 41–74. Much of this essay reappears in more elaborate form in the opening chapter of the *Political Unconscious*.
13 Hayden White, *Metahistory* (Baltimore, Md: Johns Hopkins University Press, 1973).
14 These were, of course, overlapping, and are today, simultaneous intellectual moments. My spatial form is a way of organizing these positions logically, not chronologically.
15 Let me rehearse, very schematically, these 'isms'. Descartes tells us that there are in the universe objects: or, because objects are unknowable and irreducible, that there is within thought an object category. Then there are subjects, or consciousness which, since it knows itself as such, is a primary category of knowledge and being. Subjects, which can know themselves but nothing else in any immediate and certain way, form concepts of objects: concepts partly determined by the object's active virtues (here, Descartes' paradoxically materialist *physics* interrupts his *metaphysical* idealism), and partly by the

subject's inherent and acquired mental and physiological structures. These concepts – for all purposes, representations – are radically and irremediably estranged from the objects they represent. Indeed, it is in the gap between object and representation that meaning and freedom occur. We can only form a concept of things because we cannot mentally form the thing itself. Our knowledge of things – a knowledge of our logical concepts – bears no trace of servility. Moreover, in the absence of a mechanism for reliably determining the extrinsic norm, we cannot appreciate the distortion of our thoughts.

Enlightenment materialism proposes the ontological primacy of matter and it explains whatever appears to common sense to be non-material as a manifestation, function or relational property of matter-in-motion. Knowledge consists in the translation of apparently subjective phenomena into their material reality: an ultimate code. The better the translation – a de-mystification – the greater the subject's material control and thus the fuller his freedom.

16 Alan Liu, 'The History in "Imagination"', *English Literary History*, vol. 51, (Fall 1984), pp. 505–48; '"Shapeless Eagerness": the Genre of Revolution in Books 9–10 of *The Prelude*', *Modern Language Quarterly*, vol. 43, no. 1 (March 1982), pp. 3–28; and Levinson, *Wordsworth's Great Period Poems* (Cambridge: Cambridge University Press, 1986), pp. 123ff.

17 Another way to frame this problem is as the politically serviceable reconciliation of Descartes' physics and metaphysics. See Marx, *The Holy Family*, 'French Materialism and the Origins of Socialism'.

18 Historicism managed to keep consciousness top dog, but only by making it engage matter in a particular way, one we might describe as constructive annihilation. For historicism, mind is only fully mind to the extent that it re-presents matter as a mental form. In accomplishing this reduction, mind necessarily dismantles its antithetical ground of being. In order to recover its realized subject-identity, mind – that is, the historian – must seek out new objects, new sources of alterity: literally, new material for its sublative operations. We might recognize in this formula the familiar master–slave dialectic, with the accent on matter's mastery of its master, mind. To this extent, then, we might legitimately (albeit perversely) call historicism a materialism.

19 I use 'describe' in both senses. The stories historicism tells about the past, and those it tells about the present by its own formal procedures, are both characterized by a syncretizing continuity.

20 The inter-assimilation of matter and mind is blocked at both ends. On the object side, the matter one confronts is never raw. Each transformational act is an incursion upon the traces of someone else's project, a 'someone else' structurally opposed to the projects of the present simply by his participation in a different economic formation. As for the subject, his recuperation of a humanized matter and an objectified self is impeded both by the historical antagonism of that matter, and by the alienating instruments and relations of his age. While Marx predicts, of course, historical progress through the contradictions engendered by particular modes of production, there is within his historical universe at any given moment no immediate and individual recovery through work.

21 Before outlining and, as it were, annotating my method, I'd like to cite the peculiar relevance to this argument of John Barrell's *Political Theory of Painting from Reynolds to Hazlitt* (New Haven, Conn.: Yale University Press, 1987). I came across Barrell's book long after I'd completed this essay. It must be noted, however, that the little drama I unfold here describes an episode in the extended struggle between two available rhetorics, that of traditional civic humanism and its bourgeois inflection. This struggle – its meanings, phases and forms – is Barrell's discovery.

As for the method of this reading, we begin with an extensive or progressive move; we read out from the formally disturbing textual feature – an isolated and, it would appear, unmotivated contradiction – towards a determining contextual domain which is at this point a received and relatively abstract affair. In this phase, we 'give to each [discursive] event, in addition to its particular signification, the role of being revealing' (*Search for a Method*, p. 26). By this essentially allegorical analysis, we articulate a *positionally* objective ensemble subtending the particular discursive case. By our abstractive procedures, the poem begins to assume a more situated, more concrete aspect. We now reorganize the work in the mode of 'structural difference and determinate contradiction' (Jameson, *Political Unconscious*, p. 56). In this regressive stage, what had appeared as an isolated deviation from the textual logic operates as the governing principle of the subtextual thought. By conceiving the surface–depth discrepancy as a compromise formation, we reconstruct in the form of a social problem the conditions that had to obtain for this 'solution' to take shape. Specifically, we are interested in the 'lacks and "oversignifications"' which seem to define this solution (*Search for a Method*, p. 26). We show that what is Wordsworth's is also and specifically *not* Wordsworth's: anti-Wordsworth. By bringing out that within his language which is dynamically opposed to the interests he would pursue, the negations he would accomplish, we also reveal that what is *not* his (not represented as such) is also his. Thus, even as we deconstruct his projection, we enrich it by the discourses that work alongside, within and across it. By comparing the work's private logic to the social logic that overdetermines the work's presented relations, we derive a model of internal–external, individual–social dynamics for the period in question. We use this model to reinterpret that objective ensemble installed uncritically at the outset of our criticism. (See Lukács, *The Ontology of Social Being, 2: Marx*, trans. D. Fernbach, London: Merlin, 1978, pp. 27–31.)

The method *is* circular. The particular element – a strictly apparent, unrealized concrete – is raised to the level of general, conceptual and social signification. That dimension is in turn realized – interrogated – by the particular it has engendered in the mode of difference, distance and deformation. In short, and as my rhetoric must have suggested, this two-stage exercise (progressive–regressive; reconstructive–deconstructive) is a dialectically totalizing critique. I offer it both as a methodological demonstration and more interestingly, I think, as a practical expression of the argument I've been developing.

22 Jameson, *Political Unconscious*, p. 84.
23 For 'creed' as an inscription (ironic), of Enlightened, Revolutionary values, see

'The Borderers', Act III, ll. 1213–27: spoken by Marmaduke.

24 Another insight into the negative charge hiding in that affirmation is afforded by the parallel between bosom-baring sea, line 5, and creedal 'suckling', line 10. What looks like a *return* to the generous, female, Nature-figure, line 5, is in fact a critical displacement. In *this* formal context, the wish to be a Pagan suckled in a creed outworn implies the substitution of a male, intellectual, *Greek* ideal for the fierce, passional, Roman style of the Revolutionary visual and verbal rhetorics. Liberty, that avenging Enlightenment goddess whose bared breasts signify a warrior fearlessness and independence, is imaginatively displaced by the androgynous fantasy of a nurturing 'creed'. The call-to-arms modulates into a cradling image, the female Sea becomes a 'creed' and its gift the glimpse of gods, not goddesses.

25 Jameson, *Political Unconscious*, p. 56. Jameson identifies religion as the 'shared medium or master code' in which the seventeenth century played out its ideological struggles. I propose philosophy as the nineteenth century's comparable medium of ideological articulation.

26 The reference in Wordsworth's 'Proteus coming from the sea' is to Paradise Lost III, 603–4, itself an allusion to the philosopher's stone.

27 One is meant to hear in the optative mood of the sestet a critical surpassing of the indicative and demonstrative moods of the first two sections. One is meant to experience the subjunctive, intransitive voice of the conclusion as a transcendence of the active, transitive voices of the octet.

28 I distinguish two Reals: a binary real and an absolute. By the former, I mean an order of meaning and events which the fiction defines as outside and other: in Coleridge's phrase, its 'positive negation'. By the latter, I intend Althusser's notion of the Real: that which only a belated and conceptually detoured knowledge can force out from the products of a moment organized by, and by its specific ignorance of, that Real. The first, binary real is a kind of distraction from that founding, unimaginable order.

What I develop in the following section is the concrete form which Schiller's *Formtrieb–Stofftrieb* had to assume for Wordsworth within the world of contemporary politics. It was not Wordsworth's superior insight that enabled him to comprehend the underlying identity of the dualism but his different historical position. Schiller, whose thoughts on this subject developed at the start of the Napoleonic era, could not have observed nearly so schematically as did Wordsworth, nearly a decade later, the patterns of Revolutionary reversal. He could not have observed in the realm of actual life the apparent necessity binding the liberating movement to the exploitation, the ideal and abstract materialism to the debased acquisitiveness of a particular class, the democrat to the conqueror and the conqueror to the *homme moyen sensuel*.

29 Wordsworth's Greek fantasy, a multidetermined and polyvalent affair, is at some ultimate level an attempt to imagine what we today might mean by the word 'ideology'. If we believed in such things, we might say that Wordsworth's consciousness fantasy anticipates Althusser's notion of ideology: an apparatus enabling the individual to imagine his lived relationships to the collective

social reality. At the same time, ideology thus conceived enables the individual *not* to 'live' – and here I invoke Sartre's transitive usage – his actual relation to that social domain and not to register the deprivation. We might distinguish here between those two Reals I've mentioned. Ideology produces in representational form (its only form) that Real which is the binary opposite of the age's fictive or imaginary and which must, therefore, structurally confirm that domain. At the same time, ideology obstructs that totalizing knowledge which would produce for the individuals of a particular era their objective Real: that dimension which, in our fallen world, emerges as such only retroactively, by the agency of its delayed, dissociated effect, the future.

30 See Adorno's/Horkheimer's comments on ideology as 'partisan reproduction' in *Dialectic of Enlightenment*, trans. John Cumming (New York: Continuum, 1986), p. 18; and, *Minima Moralia*, trans. E. F. N. Jephcott (London: New Left Books, 1974), pp. 209–12.

31 Wordsworth's aesthetic scholarship – his evocation of the Greeks – introduces into the poem an exemplary myth of integrated social production. Most strikingly in Shelley's work but throughout the second-generation canon, the distinctively humane consciousness of the Greeks (their arts, letters, religion) is aligned with their social formations. In reaching back to the Greeks, Wordsworth summons a genuinely utopian figure, but by the fetishistic, privatized form of the summons, he betrays the hopelessness of that gesture. His very longing for the social, for a vision of Proteus, recapitulates the logic of the placeless, privileged seer into the life of things. Thus does Wordsworth blazon his lapse from that golden age when the gods were the way individuals conceived their real relation to the collective life. Moreover, we see that Wordsworth invokes the Greeks as ideal producers of consciousness: of the gods. The representation of the social relations which engendered that consciousness is not just missing, it is figured in a certain way by its absence. One feels either that the sensibility of the Greeks saved them from a debasing exchange-dominated economy; or, that the consciousness of the Greeks *was* their material practice. Thus would we have an image of a culture that knows no distinction between mental and material labour.

One can only wonder at the terrific doubleness of these equally available meanings: these simultaneously utopian and reactionary gestures. By another irony, the utopian moment – the idea of collective production and consciousness – not only represents the corrupt Hellenism of the nineteenth century, it identifies that particular myth as the reflection of a different productive order. The sheer historicity of Wordsworth's dream precipitates the idea that turns around to expose it as a helpless reflection of contemporary life. We could say that Wordsworth's parodic translation of his critical past – the Greeks – puts that past in position to judge his translation and the age which enables it. Similarly, our critical past – Wordsworth's poem and the age it reflects – might, by this literal, parodic translation, expose the poverty of *our* dream of human life.

32 I invoke here Althusser's notion of structural causality.

33 By placing the nostalgic Hellenism of this sonnet in the context of Wordsworth's reactive nationalism (his opposition to that liberal republicanism associated with the second-generation writers and their self-consciously ideological Hellenism), we deepen the pathos of the work. Wordsworth would seem to be forced by the extremity of his own ideological binds to adopt a language – indeed, a whole affective strategy – that ran very much against his intellectual and political grain. The peculiarly suspended quality of the rhetoric – 'I'd rather be . . .' as opposed to 'I wish I were' – or what we might call its strictly comparative optatives, is perhaps illuminated by this irony. This is to say, Wordsworth's evocation of the Greeks is sentimental in both senses: self-conscious *and* ironic. I thank Elinor Shaffer and Susan Wolfson for pointing out the possibility of this reading.

I do not incorporate this reading into the body of my text for reasons that have to do with the state of the Romantic art today and with my own general attitudes towards Romantic enlightenment. The self-ironizing reading is a critical form that absorbs and discredits all alternative constructs. It is, in short, a pre-emptive move that we surely all recognize by now. And of course, the *content* of that critical form reiterates the most familiar of all the themes in the Romantic and Romanticist repertoire: the poet-critic as self-made Maker. By his critical operations on all the belief systems that enable him to think and to feel, he deconstructs himself as an ideological subject, hurling himself into the sort of post-agonic state most clearly mapped out in Baudelaire.

34 Walter Benjamin, 'The Task of the Translator', in *Illuminations*, trans. Harry Zohn, ed. Hannah Arendt (New York: Harcourt, World, Brace, 1968), pp. 69–82.

35 Here's what comes of all this shuttling. Or, here's what results from the ravishing of our textual brides. Our appreciation of the thoroughly Romantic character of Wordsworth's poem – its critical production of the past – thoroughly modernizes it. By our work, we are positioned to recognize in Wordsworth's strategies of inwardness (his opposition of the private, revelatory moment to the sordid social realities of contemporary culture), the technique of Eliot and Pound. In Wordsworth as in the high modernists, the utopian move is accomplished by and is identical with the reactionary, regressive move. The evocation of the noble past – the transparency and wholeness of the classical (i.e. pre-capitalist) cultures – is at once escape from, critique and 'ideological duplication' of the age's mean materialism. Moreover, we feel in Wordsworth, and precisely within his most humanistic longings, the same fascist edge we brush up against in Eliot and Pound: the same longing for a government that is oneself but other and that inhabits the individual as a god might do. The wish is for a creed made by human beings – an art – but one that somehow breaks free of its makers and their inevitably corrupt interests, returning to liberate them from their meanness, their guilt. This terrible dream of what Stevens calls the 'major man' is also a radical, monistic solution to the problem Sartre has defined as *the* problem of historical investigation: that of *relating* inside to outside, individual to collective life. There is, of course, a modernist *comic* solution – Joyce's, for instance – and

this is a genuine critical action. This difficult response is the dialectical rewriting of the inside–outside dualism, a response that we recognize as the desideratum of both the Marxian and Freudian hermeneutics.

2

Repossessing the Past: the Case for an Open Literary History

Marilyn Butler

In October 1986 the Cambridge historian David Cannadine informed the readers of the *Times Literary Supplement* why, broadly, he was leaving Britain for the USA. He wrote of the pointlessness of specializing in British history, now that no one but the British were interested in it.[1] In this respect scholars of past English literature look to be in a far more favourable situation than historians. The conditions affecting literature have been revolutionized from time to time. The invention of printing, the extension of literacy and leisure, the mechanization of book production, each in turn brought in new readers, and in the end the readers determine the books. We are now living through the greatest expansion yet of the reading public for serious books in English. Thanks to the world dominance of America, English is what Latin once was, a world language. By analogy, literature in English will become what the Roman Empire made Latin literature, and indeed Greek literature too. The literature in the language the world speaks is – or should be – a world literature.

But, as a matter of fact, 'literature in English' is not at all the same thing as 'English literature', in the sense that the English (or British, or those of Anglo-Saxon descent) have narrowly conceived it. Literatures in English have begun to proliferate since the late nineteenth century, in most cases accompanied by a strong will to independent nationhood, and a consciousness of linguistic particularity. The schoolchildren of Canada, Australia, Nigeria and the West Indies partly learn about national autonomy by studying cultural autonomy. They are increasingly likely to focus on their own national literatures before rather than after England's, and before rather than after America's too.

So where does that leave the 'canonical' literature of the past – Shakespeare, Milton and Wordsworth; Austen, the Brontës, George Eliot; Locke, Wortley Montagu and Ruskin; now the literature of a third-class power with a first-ranked language? The loss of British national prestige must entail a threat to the so-called authority of English literary classics – simply because the main motive for foreign children to learn about the British past, cultural as well as political, has in fact (as Cannadine perceived) been removed. Even if we suppose that America will and indeed has adopted England's literature *en bloc* as its own cultural heritage, America with its wealth and strength can afford the luxury of a cultural heritage. Will the largely third-world nations learning the language think it worth their while to follow rich Western nations on this point?

Most school students of English language are sitting, right now, at desks in China: they do not study English literature. Nations that have done so are showing signs of giving it up. Shakespeare has been for over a century on the syllabus in good Indian schools, but he is being declared too difficult, and anyhow irrelevant, and looks about to go. Schools, like universities, are in crisis where the humanities are concerned, because everywhere scarce resources are being diverted into the re-equipping, or creation, of industry. The sixties revolution that matters worldwide is not the Parisian one that gave Western academics post-structuralism, but the South Korean one that turned a war-devastated country into another Japan. The precondition of that techonological miracle was a retrained workforce, and the moral is not lost on other governments. Where education is concerned, while not precisely saying so, Britain and the United States as well as India and Australia are increasingly interested in being Korean. The British Prime Minister acknowledges the utility of studying the English language, the medium in which buying, selling, and navigating ships and planes is conducted. She seems no more impressed than Rajiv Ghandi by English literature, which sells nothing, and may carry disagreeable ideological baggage along with it.

Somewhat against their own professional interest, intelligent young Indian academic teachers of English (who are numerous) question the relevance of so much time and money spent on the past writings of a country geographically far away, which imposed this literature upon them as part of its machinery of power. Read within Britain, much of the sub-Foucauldian cultural history now pouring out of non-academic British presses – Methuen, Blackwell, Harvester, and the New Left imprint, Verso – may tend to give a crude and mechanistic account of the operation of power through literature and education. In the Third World, the iconoclasm of this type of work hearteningly confronts what otherwise looks like the white cultural monolith – for it's hard to deny the inequality of the cultural exchange between north and west on the one hand, south and east on the other. The bright young staff of Delhi University, readers of their own *Subaltern Studies* and of Gayatri Spivak's *In Other Worlds*, as well as of the brisk cheap left-wing semi-academic Western paperbacks, are provisionally willing enough to tolerate the canon, because they are so accomplished at turning it into cannon-fodder: apt material for a brutal, totalizing, highly political form of deconstruction, owing little to the manner of Yale and Cornell.

Aggressive manoeuvres of that kind, whether or not tactically appropriate in the Third World, are surely not good or even interesting choices for readers studying their own native tradition, or working in their own first language. We have all severally to work out our own models for how literary history is to be taught in our different countries. It must be for many of us a brutal simplification, and in the end a self-destructive one, to type all past literature as the voice of power, or of patriarchy, or of any other hateful institution. This form of pessimism or 'tragic essentialism', as it has been termed, is self-defeating because it glamorizes what it means to oppose. And a tactic devoted to exposing the bad faith of literature as a whole is hardly timely when, throughout much of the world, time and resources spent on research in the humanities have come under severe scrutiny from the central state. Yet this reductive position, under-researched, pseudo-intellectual, is able to pass professionally as a 'historical' approach to literature, for want of enough properly rigorous alternatives. At least the seriousness of the situation should belatedly force more ambitious literary critics to pay attention to the kind of issue that in the Romantic-modernist period they have characteristically evaded – the question of the relationship between culture and the state; more specifically, the role and rationale of past literature in education.

It can't be much more than 400 years since the centralized nation-states of Western Europe such as England began to cultivate their own pasts, including their vernacular literary pasts, as a means of raising national consciousness. For about half that time, the first 200 years or so, those who took a 'patriot' pride in native English (and in Scottish and Welsh) literatures were often not nationalists, in the modern sense of rallying behind the nation's leaders. From the seventeenth century on, amateurs among the gentry and middling sort collected vernacular books or the ephemera of popular culture. Pepys's huge collection of ballads, now in Magdalene College, Cambridge, has recently been published, and it illustrates the appeal of native alternatives to the aristocratic classical tradition. When the House of Commons debated the future of Latin in November 1987, the British public heard heartfelt references to 3,000 years of European culture. The same line of legitimacy was invoked in the eighteenth century to justify that period's truly conspicuous consumption in the arts – in architecture, or in classical statuary. But the classical heritage was articulately contested by other people's traditions. The new middle-class journals, with their largely provincial readership, encouraged the emergence of a more British, non-Latinate literary past, including ballads, Gothic tales, Elizabethan lyric and drama, and (for the learned like Cambridge's Thomas Gray) Anglo-Saxon, Celtic and Old Norse. The eighteenth-century writers who claimed that literature was originally simple and spontaneous were not themselves especially simple, and some of them invented their evidence, but they got what they wanted from history by remaking it. That generation, as well as the Victorian, is one of our possible models.

A single, official English literary history emerges only in the 1820s. The monoliths which European nation-states then made of their cultural traditions are deeply impressive, since they served all sorts of civic purposes, from mass literacy to nationalism, while remaining usefully economical. Critics around 1830 made the single great line of English poets, stretching (almost) unbroken from Chaucer to Tennyson. The so-called literary canon, a significantly theological term, was as characteristic of the age of its birth as the railway, and as much the symbol of British achievement. Together the single line of poets personified the national spirit, separately they were thoughtful, humane men – a little too like the ideal university professor, perhaps, but wisdom and tolerance remain virtues. Wordsworth emerged *primus inter pares* among the other five Romantics – then Coleridge, Scott, Byron, Shelley, Keats – because he taught a stoical, essentially optimistic acceptance of suffering, and because his vision of nature represented England as still a pastoral society, which was comforting in other ways.

The impact of the canon on all our perceptions is perhaps most striking when we reflect how quickly and how totally it changed posterity's understanding of the two literary generations before its acceptance. In the age of Adam Smith, large numbers of general readers were able to buy or borrow books for the first time. The novels and poems offered to these new readers were often quotidian in their concerns, and direct, non-specialized in their vocabulary and range of allusion. Many authors were women; some of the best poets, we might now agree – like Burns and Blake – came from the ranks. Nineteenth-century professionals, journalists and academics, made great writers into an officer class, and imposed restrictions on the entry of women and NCOs. The canon came to look harmonious rather than contentious; learned or polite rather than artless or common; national, rather than provincial or sectarian on the one hand, or dispersed and international on the other. Literature is individualistic or pluralist; words such as 'canon' and 'heritage' impose a uniformity that had some practical advantages, especially at the outset, but was always artificial.

The Victorian canon must have been made for the 'general reader', more for consumption at home than in the classroom, since the process of canon-making clearly predates the rise of English Literature as a school and university subject. By the second half of the nineteenth century, the era of mass secondary education, syllabus reform and the provision of academic school and university places for women, English literature was already so wholesome a field of study that its social utility was easy to argue for. Victorians, noted for their hardheadedness, saw the merits of a school subject that delivered the nation's traditions to pupils in an inspiring, unifying and easily digested form. On the most practical level, it provided models for using the language, most universal of all skills in advanced society; it opened the door to experience, personal and social, in the adult world. Given the large and steadily increasing numbers of women studying the subject, the supply of teachers was unlikely to run short. All these arguments still prevail, and are being rehearsed again in Britain, as a reforming government strives for an education system which will deliver, among other things, a mentally disciplined, trainable workforce. But what will the content of that school literature syllabus be? Must it still resemble the Victorian conception, simply because the Victorian conception is there?

The nature of the population has, after all, changed a great deal in a century. It is now more urbanized and more ethnically diverse, and many of the non-formal aspects of its culture are new (radio, television, film, tabloid newspapers, sport). The adult work required of the populace in the twenty-first century will be very different from that required in the nineteenth. Without an empire to hold down, there seems less point in schooling young males in hearty nationalism (though many believers in educational reform still seem very keen on breeding patriots). There is, on the other hand, a valuable social lesson just as cogently drawn from studying past literature, that of learning to understand and tolerate the other person's position. Most literature does not speak for the official, London-based 'nation'. It expresses the view of a sect, a province, a gender, a class, bent more often than not on criticism or outright opposition. For literary purposes, the British Isles have always been what the Australian poet Les Murray recently termed them in the present day, 'the Anglo-Celtic archipelago'. As a social institution, literature models an intricate, diverse, stressful community, not a bland monolith.

There is now a logical and powerful case against mindlessly adopting any canon of great works as a basis for teaching literature in schools. It's hard not to smuggle in inappropriate ideas about what is most permissible, best sanctioned by an invisible, unexaminable 'authority'. And we have to acknowledge that reading a book sets up a transaction between author and reader, changing all the time as readers change. The consultation document which the Department of Education and Science in London sent out in July 1987 on the proposed new National Curriculum wisely acknowledged that its content must depend on who the pupils are now and where they have come from. We should ensure, it says, 'that all pupils, regardless of sex, ethnic origin and geographical location, have access to broadly the same good and relevant curriculum and programmes of study'. True, it goes on to speak of a body of pre-existent knowledge, the 'key content, skills and processes which they need to learn'. But it also respects 'relevance to the pupils' own experience' and 'continuing value to adult and working life'. Every pupil has a right to be given access to as much refined, musical poetry, as many great dramas and novels, as they can read with pleasure and profit to themselves. But that principle also implies a willingness to experiment with other materials, works of hitherto non-canonical status, which individual pupils, or minorities of pupils, would find more profitable. That is the syllabus problem as it affects schools, and it is in fact the greater and more pressing problem, with its own long-term repercussions on the teaching of literature in universities. But I want now to turn to look at the problem from the other end, not as a pedagogic issue in schools, but as an intellectual issue forced upon academics by radically changed modern circumstances. How in principle should we define the content of English Literature? How meet the objection that its existing normal content emerged at a particular time, for particular reasons, many of which no longer apply?

There is also a formidable case against continuing with the Victorian canon in its depleted modern version, as the basis either for teaching university students or for pursuing literary research. Over time the canon seems to have acquired a weird momentum of its own, and to have introduced various restrictive practices into criticism. Some originally pragmatic choices acquired fixity because, by the mid twentieth century, if you are a dead author and not in the canon you are probably not in print. The number of poets one *must* study gets fewer, and the number of poems by each writer gets much fewer, as time goes on. The questions that can be asked of major figures dwindle in number and importance with the fading of minor ones. The relations between texts are always of crucial significance, but it was left to twentieth-century scholars to claim that only major texts and major authors have meaningful relations. Keats now communes too often with Shakespeare, Wordsworth with St Augustine, everyone with the Bible. However much an artist is indebted to the mighty dead, he or she almost certainly borrows more from the living – that is, from writers no longer available for reading except in the better libraries. In the end, evaluation itself is threatened: how can you operate the techniques for telling who a major writer is, if you don't know what a minor one looks like?

Even in its adjusted modern form, the canon is being rapidly overtaken by events. Already within the last generation some academics at Columbia, Yale and Cornell have been redrafting literary history, while often denying that there is a literary history worth studying. M. H. Abrams, Geoffrey Hartman, Harold Bloom and their colleagues and pupils, encouraged by the Canadian Northrop Frye, have quietly installed their own line, which gives the modern East-coast intellectual his own appropriate intellectual genealogy, and is also, perhaps accidentally, conterminous with the independent history of the United States of America.

This line begins with Kant and runs through Blake, Wordsworth, Coleridge, Shelley to Hegel, Emerson, Carlyle, Whitman, Nietzsche, Freud and Wallace Stevens. German thinkers play a large part in the New England canon; many of the academics constructing it seem to have spoken German as their first language, and to have trained in traditions that gave them no such personal motives for Anglophilia as old-style Ivy League professors often had. Since America has always been a multi-ethnic community, the British-built canon must often have tended to alienate, or at least fail to inspire, many of its students of literature. The strategic placing of Americans in the new one, and the skilful modernizing of the consciousnesses of the figures in it, does away, at first sight, with two of the more repellent features of old Eng. Lit. – its foreignness, and its historicity. On the other hand, it must be said that the new Modernist-Romantic canon hardly looks tailor-made for students: it is still Eurocentric and intimidatingly learned, through its range of allusion to the 2,000-year Hebraic religious tradition which the English Romantics allegedly revived. Wealth and prestige within the American university system continues to shift to California: it will be an interesting test of the responsiveness of the profession in America, to see if Emersonian New England gradually allows a pitch in the avant-garde parkland to California's Hispanics and Chinese.

It would be premature to offer rival international or British inner-city canons: those have to emerge with time, and with the raising of the consciousness of those currently marginalized. But an individual academic can at least begin to explore the unfortunate intellectual consequences of letting a small set of survivors, largely accidentally arrived at, dictate the model many of us seem to work with, of a timeless, desocialized, ahistorical literary community. What kind of critical difference would it make to study actual literary communities as they functioned within their larger communities in time and place? I propose that poets we have installed as canonical look more interesting individually, and far more understandable as groups, when we restore some of their lost peers. My example is a poet who was not accidentally overlooked but dropped by the curious consensus-making of the 1820s, for he was the Poet Laureate of the day, Robert Southey.

In 1802, when Wordsworth was already at the peak of his powers, Southey was greeted by Francis Jeffrey as the leader of a 'sect of dissenters' from literature's established conventions, to which Wordsworth merely belonged.[2] What produced this rapid and it seems permanent reversal in the two poets' fortunes? The modern critic will confidently say that their relative status has been properly fixed by our assessment of their power to handle language, but other factors counted for more at the outset. Southey possessed non-canonical qualities – he was contentious rather than reassuring, common rather than genteel, provincial rather than metropolitan, international rather than national. And he was no solitary or recluse, amenable to study out of context, as the more favoured Wordsworth and Keats were; he engaged actively with his contemporaries, and they with him. I think it will begin to seem more natural to us in the future to replace the old thin line of national heroes with a richer and more credible notion: that, because writers represent groups and attitudes within the community, they come dynamically into contention with one another. They accordingly lose much of their vitality, their strongest, most urgent meanings, when read without the antagonists with whom they contend – the writers found formidable in their own generation, even if excised in ours. Southey's restoration to the Romantics at once makes them look more like a real group, which can be examined for evidence of how a strong movement of poetry – that most exalted and eloquent form of social intercommunication – actually works.

Southey was a Bristolian, and a provincial patriot. Like the Bristol poet of the previous generation, Thomas Chatterton, he believed in popular and local cultural traditions. He was a more conventional scholar than Chatterton, meaning that he did not invent documentary evidence for the existence of these traditions. He contented himself with reanimating them for his own times, publishing imitations of ballads under his own name in 1797 and 1799. Some were of the medieval type, often comic or lightly satirized; others used the still-current broadside ballad convention of commenting on public affairs. It was because Southey's friendship with Coleridge was common knowledge that Francis Jeffrey could damn the *Lyrical Ballads* and Wordsworth, by association, as disaffected.

Southey was also fascinated by the wider world with which Bristol traded, and by the European diaspora into East and West. While still at school in the 1780s, he said he was going to write a poem in the manner of the mythology of every major religious system. The first to appear, and my example of the marginalized writing we have lost – another poem to read, calling on other ways of reading – is the 'Islamic' romance *Thalaba* (1801). The nearest model to this poem in Western literature would be the fanciful, magical Renaissance epics of Ariosto, Tasso and Spenser, surprisingly courtly models for the faintly scurrilous balladeer. On closer inspection, Southey's vulgar materials are found to be still there – *Thalaba* is a cunning anthology of good stories from East and West, old books and travellers' tales. Later editions sometimes drop the often comic or scurrilous notes, and then the poem looks altogether more elevated and respectable, an allegorical tale about a knight's journey to find and do battle with the powers of evil. It is far more rewarding to read the original, unexpurgated version than the one which accommodated Victorian taste.

Thalaba begins, somewhere in Arabia, with a murder. The victim is Hodeirah, surprised and slaughtered while sleeping in his tent along with most of his children, though his wife and one young son, Thalaba, manage to escape. The murderers are a band of wicked magicians whom we meet next in their Underworld kingdom, Domdaniel. There, by means of some explicit, bloodthirsty and compulsively readable black magic, they find out that their attack has been only partially successful: they must trace Thalaba and kill him, or he is destined to destroy them. It is a familiar enough plot to those who know *Macbeth*. Meanwhile Thalaba, by now also motherless, is adopted by a virtuous Bedouin, Moath. He grows up a simple nomad and a herdsman, a preparation, like Abraham's and Mohammed's, for a life of exemplary religious heroism.

By the fourth book Thalaba is old enough to go out in search of his father's enemies, who are equally keen to find him. The middle part of the poem shows him being tested in a series of discrete stories, all of which must put the reader in mind of other narratives out of the whole course of symbolic and fantastic literature, high and low. He is tempted in the desert; he journeys to the gates of the Underworld; he visits an apparent paradise of pleasure and delight, which he sees through as a worldly fake, and destroys. From that false but wonderful valley created by the enchanter Aloadin, Thalaba rescues his foster-sister Oneiza. When the two are welcomed and rewarded by a neighbouring king, Thalaba, forgetting his quest, seizes the opportunity to marry. Against Oneiza's advice, he invites guests to the wedding party. That night Azrael, the Angel of Death, visits the house and takes the bride.

Something very like this fatal wedding party occurs in two later Romantic works, Mary Shelley's *Frankenstein* and Keats's *Lamia*. Equally, the visit to the Underworld two books earlier rings a bell: we know it from remarkably similar journeys through underground caverns in later prose fantasies like George Macdonald's in the late nineteenth century, or J. R. R. Tolkien's in the twentieth. These are examples of Southey's extraordinary intertextual range, his *vulgarity*, in the strict senses that he's both thoroughly absorbed with popular art, and himself the medium by which traditional stories make their way down into the cultural water-table, to spring up oddly in (say) the pages of Rider Haggard's *She* or *King Solomon's Mines*, or in other popular locations. Thalaba goes mad when he thinks his dead wife Oneiza is coming back each night to taunt him with failure. The apparition is exposed as a vampire, who can be killed only by driving a stake through her heart. Many a Victorian shocker, culminating in Bram Stoker's *Dracula*, can trace its genealogy back to this episode via Byron – who used it sensationally in his poem *The Giaour*, with acknowledgements in the notes to Southey.

Released in Book VIII from the last of his worldly ties, Thalaba sets off into wintry landscapes, a high, cold and pure terrain which matches his new ascetic frame of mind. The journey into cold places contains the best scenes in the poem – best of all, a marvellous little folktale which begins when he comes frozen to a cave to find an old woman spinning in the light of her fire:

> The pine boughs they blazed chearfully,
> And her face was bright with the flame;
> Her face was as a Damsel's face,
> And yet her hair was grey.
> She bade him welcome with a smile,
> And still continued spinning,
> And singing as she spun.
> The thread the Woman drew
> Was finer than the silkworm's,
> Was finer than the gossamer;
> The song she sung was low and sweet,
> And Thalaba knew not the words . . .
>
> The youth sate watching it [the thread]
> And she beheld his wonder.
> And then again she spake,
> And still her speech was song:
> 'Now twine it round thy hands I say,
> Now twine it round thy hands I pray,
> My thread is small, my thread is fine,
>   But he must be
>   A stronger than thee,
> Who can break this thread of mine!'
>
> And up she rais'd her bright blue eyes,
> And sweetly she smil'd on him,
> And he conceiv'd no ill . . .
> And up she rais'd her bright blue eyes,
> And sweetly she smil'd on him,
> 'I thank thee, I thank thee, Hodeirah's son!
> I thank thee for doing what can't be undone,
> For binding thyself in the chain I have spun!'
>   (*Thalaba*, Book VIII)[3]

Southey's experimental metres can be troublesome in narrative.

They come into their own here, and in the incantatory curse in his *Curse of Kehama*, two passages where the inspiration is the charm, a particularly simple type of English folk verse. Partly because the metre sounds authentic, this scene and its sequel, where the witch Maimuna's horrific sister appears, become believable on their own terms. They suspend not so much disbelief as the automatic superior prestige of forms and metres from the corpus of polished written literature. They even evoke the uncanny, a rare achievement in eighteenth-century poetry.

After his escape from Maimuna the witch, by a mechanism of plot I would not dream of giving away, Thalaba eventually finds a little boat, with another mysterious woman at the helm, in which he travels down a stream, which becomes a river, and finally a great sea. It is, as Southey's note observes, a classic allegory for human life: Shelley was to borrow that boat and that allegory in poem after poem. At the end of his journey Thalaba makes his own way down into the caverns of Domdaniel, the kingdom at the roots of the ocean – which, Samson-like, he brings down on his own head and on the heads of his enemies.

Southey's poem is a learned anthology of the popular, or rather of what the Enlightenment littérateur made of the popular. Its experimental unrhymed stanza is based on half a century of work by others. Lowth on the poetry of the Bible, Gray on Pindar and on Norse and Welsh poetry, Macpherson on Gaelic poetry, all tried to recapture the forms as well as the essential spirit of the very earliest verse. Arab primitive poetry was, as the great Orientalist Sir William Jones said, simple and passionate and thus the essence of true poetry. But Southey, like other Enlightenment historicists, was never a passive revivalist or antiquarian. He was a polemicist, and above all, at this time, a student of the Rousseau who wrote the *Second Discourse, On the Origins and Foundations of Inequality among Men*, in which the sketch of a stylized primitive state prior to civilization is also the blueprint for an ideal republic yet to be attained.

Following Rousseau's analysis of the 'progress', or rather degeneration, of civilization, Southey used another Arab literary tradition known in the West, magical courtly tales of the *Arabian Nights* type. Through them he portrays a more advanced period, corresponding with the European middle ages, when pure religion became credulous and subject to the machinations of wicked priests (the magicians of the plot of *Thalaba*). Southey's notes to his worldly mid-poem section multiply examples of superstition, and subject them to his own sardonic comparativist commentary. 'Monkish ingenuity has invented something not unlike the Mohammedan article of faith . . .' (note to Book IX).[4] Mohammedanism now resembles Roman Catholicism, a religion Southey associates with forms of despotism still extant in Europe. His poem allegorizes not an individual life, but Everyman travelling through time and through stages of culture which are the same worldwide. The hero leaves his pastoral origins for a corrupt advanced society, which he overthrows, restoring the primal simplicity by force. Small wonder that Jeffrey when reviewing *Thalaba* was put in mind of 'the sage of Geneva', Rousseau, in his most tendentious vein.[5]

When in the spring of 1800 Southey set off for Portugal to write *Thalaba*, he took with him *The Ancient Mariner*, by his friend Coleridge, from whom he was temporarily estranged. Southey had already denounced *The Ancient Mariner* in an anonymous review as a profoundly inauthentic imitation of a ballad;[6] *Thalaba* shows better than the review what the grounds of that criticism were. Particularly near the beginning and end, Southey's poem repeatedly brings to mind Coleridge's poem, inviting comparison, setting up a dialogue between the two. Thalaba's nobility is established by his kindness to an animal, his camel, as it dies of thirst in the desert. Here, and in an inset story in Book I with a similar theme, Southey plainly introduces parallels to the slaying of the albatross, but he simultaneously invokes a poem by Coleridge in more humanitarian vein, his early, much-ridiculed *Address to a Young Ass*.[7] The highly stylized and allegorical boat journey at the end of Southey's poem is achieved 'without an oar, without a sail', in Coleridge's rhythms and imagery. By enforcing his parallels at the beginning and end of his hero's journey, Southey draws attention to his protagonist's greater purposefulness. As a result the two plots relate very differently to the notion of progression.

For Southey, the onward momentum of the action implies, as we have seen, the passing of time; progression necessarily introduces the idea of progress. Southey the Rousseauist and secularist sees culture as man-made, evolutionary, but also capable of being changed by human will: revolutionary change becomes possible, change itself desirable. When Coleridge imitates the writings of the past, he repeats their attitudes as well as their forms; change is slowed down, less significant than continuity. *The Ancient Mariner* is no less historically conscious than *Thalaba*. It constantly uses the individual voices of the past, either by quoting them directly, or by letting alien words and phrases stray into the text, as fossils crop up in strata of rocks. The mariners credulously and inconsistently interpret the albatross as a bird of good and evil omen. The pilot, his boy, the Wedding Guest, interpret the Mariner himself. As enlightened readers, we know that yet more unidentified minds have intervened in the story we have. The Mariner, presumably illiterate, must have told it early in the sixteenth century. Someone who heard it, other than the Wedding Guest, wrote it down, on linguistic evidence not much later. A much more learned editor added marginal glosses at least a century after that, and thus the academic discourse of Jeremy Taylor's day inserts itself into the popular narrative. The changes Coleridge made to his poem over nearly twenty years confirm its suggestive appearance, as a text submitting to change, a witness to the processes of history.

This marked, sophisticated interest in a text's own material nature was highly typical of the later eighteenth century. Less predictable was Coleridge's attitude to the transmission of cultural artefacts, his resigned or detached acceptance of all contributions as *natural* – for this evidently seemed new and displeasing to Southey, his former partner and senior colleague in the field of folk culture. The story follows the path simple seamen alive in 1500 would have imagined for it: divine retribution follows the slaying of the albatross. Neutrals, the hermit and the pilot, see the arrival of the ship sailed by the ghastly crew. The more sophisticated seventeenth-century additions do nothing to de-mystify the Mariner's oral version, but on the contrary piously adorn what is, in fact, a smoothly evolving record of faith, the 'panharmonium' of the universal church in which Coleridge believed. He is imitating in smaller compass the construction of the greatest sacred text, the Bible, by many witnesses in different places in different times. By omitting the *hostile* textual criticism of the Bible and other sacred texts in the *philosophe* tradition, he seems to endorse Burke's attack on French revolutionary ideologues and their British sympathizers: modern sceptics may not validly reinterpret these events, these experiences, this customary understanding. Coleridge denies that possibility Southey envisages in *Thalaba*, of a break in the hermeneutic circle of believers, or a break-out from preconditioned mentalities.

Thalaba, one of the first Romantic poems to narrate a spiritual quest, is also a critique of such quests. Though *The Ancient Mariner* and perhaps *Kubla Khan*[8] are the deliberately revivalist romances with which Southey openly takes issue, implicitly he also has much to say to Wordsworth, whose *Prelude* is nowadays hailed as the greatest of all Romantic quest poems. Wordsworth's first version of his autobiography was written in two books in 1799: here Wordsworth is preoccupied with boyhood experiences, and with his growth, guided by Nature, into consciousness and conscience. Two years later *Thalaba* appeared, a strong poetic representation of an entire life; two years after that, in 1803, Southey moved to the Lake District and became for the first time Wordsworth's regular associate. Wordsworth did not say that he found *Thalaba* exemplary, and was unlikely to do so after Jeffrey had termed him a mere follower in Southey's sect. Yet by 1805 he has changed *The Prelude* so that, for the first time, he as its simple country-born protagonist lives through a full epic action, beginning with the worldly temptations of Cambridge, descending to the hell-on-earth of London, and ending with a visionary experience on a mountain-top. This, the least well-documented of *Thalaba*'s intertextual relations, is potentially the most notable.

The one fully acknowledged great disciple of Southey was Shelley, who claimed to know large parts of *Thalaba* and *Kehama* by heart from his schooldays. In 1812 Shelley, then twenty, visited Southey in the Lakes, and was disappointed to find that the author of *Thalaba* had dwindled into a mere ex-radical. For Shelley's poetry disillusionment came too late. Again and again, his favourite devices, his allegorical journeys and mythological landscapes, plainly derive from Southey. *The Witch of Atlas*, a late poem written in 1820, uses a firelit cave where the witch spins, a voyage in a supernatural boat and another through the air in a car, all features so stamped with Shelley's signature that few nowadays think of them as first Southey's. They are images usable by both poets because they suit their favourite allegorical plot, the journey as metaphor both for a single life and for human progress.

But Shelley's early poetry also reverts to the defection of a man who in 1813 became Poet Laureate. *Queen Mab*, *The Revolt of Islam*, and especially *Alastor* (1816) assail *Thalaba* and *The Curse of Kehama* as directly as *Thalaba* contends with *The Ancient Mariner*. *Alastor* is Shelley's ironic 'collective biography' of the Lake poets, who had so grievously disappointed him in the last two years by their published rejoicings over the defeat of France. In the prose Preface to *Alastor* and in its final verse paragraph Shelley foregrounds Wordsworth among his targets by quoting him. Otherwise the poem looks towards Southey, since it impressionistically repeats the plot of *Thalaba*. Shelley's protagonist, a self-proclaimed 'visionary', begins by scrabbling among Gothic horrors. He sets off, leaving an Arab maiden who loves him, to fulfil a high, celibate destiny. He struggles onwards and upwards into arid, cold places, assisted at one point by a magic boat which Mary Shelley in her *Posthumous Works* of Shelley says is from *Thalaba*. But there is no achievement, no consummation, in Shelley's version of the quest, because he equates the turning-point of the plot of *Thalaba*, the moment when Thalaba turns away from the memory of his dead bride to go up into the mountains, with the abandonment of human ties and of worldly goals (such as revolution). Deluded from first to last, Shelley's Poet, his parodic Thalaba, dies among the rocks.

Southey's great antagonist and greatest debtor is Byron, who made his name using Southey's form, the annotated narrative poem; his setting, in the middle east; and his implied subject-matter, which Byron along with Shelley and Tom Moore, as author of *Lalla Rookh*, understood very well. It is Southey who gives the younger Romantics their great theme: the empires of the world and their imagined overthrow, picturesquely rendered. Byron often takes scenes and ideas from *The Curse of Kehama* (1810), in which Southey gives a violently unfavourable account of Hinduism. The two opening scenes of this poem must be the most frequently repeated scenes in Romantic literature. In the first book, the two young widows of an evil Hindu prince are burnt alive on his funeral pyre; in the second, the rajah Kehama condemns a peasant to a frightful punishment, eternal life during which his heart will burn forever. Southey's point is that Hinduism is a cruel, politicized religion, the tool of hereditary rulers. When Byron and Shelley parody these scenes, they lay the guilt for the cruelty and despotism at the door of Christians, as highly placed as possible. God the

Father curses the Wandering Jew in *Queen Mab*, our mother Eve quotes Southey's very words to curse her son in *Cain*.

Southey would have been of value to Byron and Shelley merely as the villain they set him up to be – the turncoat who became the Establishment's official poet. Partly because Southey's scenic skills invite plagiarism and parody, their poems are implicated with his as with no other poet's. But the relationship with Southey is most interesting for being visibly vexatious to the younger poets. While Southey becomes a supporter of government, especially over the preservation of order in India and at home, he also remains a populist. The hero and heroine of *The Curse of Kehama* (1810), a Hindu peasant and his daughter, recall Thalaba the herdsman, and the two protagonists of Southey's revolutionary youth, Wat Tyler and Joan of Arc. Byron and Shelley claimed to react adversely to the Hindu epic because, by calling for a kind of reformation in India, it implicitly justified British empire-building there. Yet Southey's representation of society within India might be construed as humanitarian, egalitarian and socially radical. It is after all the Indian peasants, not the gods, and not 'liberators' from overseas, who challenge and overthrow the 'Brahminical' old order.

Shelley and Byron, who are keen through their poetry to promote revolution abroad, say less about it at home. They seem to have the aristocrat's reluctance to admit vulgar people into heroic stories and into poetry, even as revolutionaries. Byron, whose imagined uprisings are more specifically placed than Shelley's, always puts strangers, often western Europeans, at the head of these skirmishes: men of mysterious origins who could by common fictional convention turn out to be princes in disguise. And though Byron puts patriotic songs into his longer poems, and even casts part of *The Giaour* as a tavern tale, he does not imitate vulgar verse-forms, or let his voice drop to the lower registers of culture.

The recent American Romanticist orthodoxy declares the great Romantic topic to be the alienated individual consciousness; the great work, Wordsworth's *Prelude*, that autobiography of a post-revolutionary recluse. As we have seen, this makes Romanticism specially and newly relevant to displaced academics, experiencing alienation from American society, and perhaps experiencing it from British society as read through literature. The impulse of such critics to exalt a few works extravagantly is often justified as the effort to teach the young that there are values higher than those taught by a crass commercial culture. The innovations of the Romantics indeed amount, for M. H. Abrams, to a 'displaced theology'.[9] But the heroic ideal being extracted from Romantic poetry – the way of the literate recluse – is far too privileged and – dare one suggest – too professionally interested, to seem truly universal. It needs not ousting but supplementing, with forms of poetry and novels that are serious and intelligent without so often being private and academic.

Literature lives by seeming to express the experiences and interests of its readers. Romantic poets convey alienation (some of the time), but they also treat group and national experience in what was already, recognizably, the modern world. As a group they can be seen to deal with social change – with the need for it, or with its costs. They weigh religious explanations of the past against scientific explanations. They prophesy the future, which they know is to be achieved by imagining it: the very project of culture in an age of literacy and mass education. If the treatment of the past by Romantic writers is always so selective and tendentious, it is because they are busy seizing their chance to shape the future.

Inevitably they take different sides, rewriting similar narratives in order to challenge or refute one another. Blake, Southey, Byron and Shelley are conscious internationalists. Wordsworth on the other hand is an English patriot, and Keats tactically avoids geographical precision, in a world recently so fought over that place-names have political implications. The British Victorians preferred the more English, less international and less revolutionary Wordsworth and Keats; American neo-Romanticists similarly play down those poems and those poets that force us to remember the current international scene, the violent and intrusive 'world'.

If *Thalaba* and *Kehama* were to be acknowledged as texts the group itself took to be central, the allegorical plot they share with *The Prelude* would be seen to have other, less private implications; in its context, even the privacy of *The Prelude* is challenged and threatened. The purposeful journey, nowadays tendentiously spiritualized through being designated a 'quest', could equally well be read as a plot characteristically signifying revolution, its re-enactments, its threatened return. Southey's *Thalaba the Destroyer* (along with immediate precursor poems such as Landor's *Gebir*, 1798, and Campbell's *Pleasures of Hope*, 1799) develops the narrative symbolic of revolution, on such terms that it is no longer confined to France, or to Europe, or to the literal revolutions of the immediate past. After Landor's *Gebir* and Southey's *Thalaba*, the location of the imagined coming struggles shifts from Europe into the empires of the East – empires then ruled, in real life, by decaying Turkey and expansive Britain. Exotic Romanticism, so-called escapist Romanticism – those forays into the Third World which the academic consensus has so long deemed marginal – may prove to have a place (in current educational parlance) at the core of our subject after all.

Some literary relationships are marvellously nuanced: it's the glory of twentieth-century criticism to have uncovered a network of echoes, verbal allusions, minimalist quotations, that both establishes poetry as a rich private language, and seals it off from more prosaic public discourse. Other types of relationship between poets, flagrant, parodic, contentious, were meant to be read in the public sphere, and these, paradoxically, have become almost too large to see. Southey's relations with his contemporaries were of the latter kind, and the key to them lies in his populism, which I've called his vulgarity. The dialogue he sets up most typically expresses itself not as variations of diction, but as variations of plot; and plot, a more democratic language, readily suggests real-life correlatives – change, action, revolt.

Admitting Southey to the canon we have grown used to studying would not be a matter of enlarging it by one name. Several of the best-regarded poems of mainstream Romanticism interrelate so significantly with Southey's poems that they are no longer quite the same read without them. But if this is so, Southey's awkward status, neither canonical nor invisible to us, queries the formalist belief in the autonomous great poem, as well as the 'post-Romantic' faith in the independence of the great poet. Southey's position on the outside of the canon also raises the less palatable implications of that institution as a metaphor: it makes poets look like an exclusive club, an aristocracy, an old regime, a leadership of the righteously inclined.

Politics and the social needs of the day (progressive quite as much as oppressive) created in the nineteenth century these notions of literature, which history has delivered to us. It will be politics and new social needs that now induce us to revise them. The consequences of shirking a revision are great, for the opportunity facing teachers of literature in our lifetime may not recur in the next generation. Should millions of potential readers of great literature, in all parts of the world, be welcomed or repelled, given access to the past or in effect denied it? The barriers raised in their path at present include the intellectual and imaginative limitations, the conservativism or the possessiveness or the downright parochialism of entrenched literary professionals. A new historicism, newer and more open than most work attracting that description at present, seems a far healthier option.

Notes

A version of this chapter was first given as a lecture at Cambridge on 10 November 1987, under the title 'Literature as a Heritage: or Reading Other Ways', and reprinted by Cambridge University Press, © 1988.

1. D. Cannadine, 'What Hope for British History?', *Times Literary Supplement*, 10 October 1986, pp. 1139–40.
2. Review of Southey's *Thalaba the Destroyer*, *Edinburgh Review*, 1 (1802), p. 63.
3. *Thalaba*, 2nd edn, 2 vols (London: Longman, 1809), vol. II, pp. 89–92.
4. Ibid., vol. II, p. 159.
5. 'Southey's *Thalaba*', p. 63.
6. '*The Lyrical Ballads*', *Critical Review*, October 1798.
7. To draw attention to Coleridge's ass was ostentatious, since that poem was the reason Southey and Coleridge appeared together with asses' heads in 'The New Morality', Gillray's celebrated caricature of leftist intellectuals in *The Anti-Jacobin* (1798).
8. For the relations between *Thalaba* and *Kubla Khan*, see my 'Plotting the Revolution: Romanticism as Political Narrative', in *Romantic Revolutions: Criticism and Theory*, ed. Kenneth R. Johnston (Bloomington: University of Indiana Press, forthcoming).
9. *Natural Supernaturalism* (New York: Norton, 1971), p. 68.

3
The Third World of Criticism

Jerome McGann

> There is no freedom, even for masters, in the midst of slaves.
> Byron

At the conclusion of his great essay 'Concerning Violence' Frantz Fanon argues that 'The fate of the world depends upon' whether the first two worlds, and especially the first world, are able to operate from a non-colonialist imagination.[1] To Fanon this means that the first world must be forced to realize its obligation not merely to allow the Third World its independent development, but also to assist actively in that development, and with no strings attached.

The full argument is by this time a familiar one, though certainly no less important for that reason. What still surprises a Western reader of this essay is its exclusive rhetoric. Fanon's essay addresses the people of the Third World; indeed, not until the conclusion does he allow himself to think at all about the effect his words might have on the first two worlds. But at the end, for the first time in the essay, the people from those other two worlds are allowed in the room with Fanon and his audience, are allowed to listen, from the margin of Fanon's centre, to the urgency of his message.

What we hear, from our corner of that room, is 'what [the Third World] expects from those who for centuries have kept it in slavery'. The message is 'to rehabilitate mankind, and make man victorious, once and for all':

> This huge task which consists of reintroducing mankind into the world, the whole of mankind, will be carried out with the indispensable help of the European peoples, who themselves must realize that

in the past they have often joined the ranks of our common masters where colonial questions were concerned. To achieve this the European peoples must first decide to wake up and shake themselves, use their brains, and stop playing the stupid game of Sleeping Beauty.[2]

From the vantage of the eavesdropping 'European peoples' – ourselves – this involves awakening from certain luxurious and heroic dreams. We are to stop projecting those grand illusions that proceed from small imaginations. If we are hearing Fanon at all we are hearing from his point of view – that is to say, from the point of view of a Third World, where the dialectic of the first two worlds is completely reimagined.

The problem here is not at all that we occupy a *different* world, but that in investing it with privilege we have generated the inertias of violence and domination that Fanon has spoken of. Nor is the problem simply that our heritage of violence has borne away an actual Third World. The problem is more acute, simple and closer to home: that in our violent histories we have acquired a certain kind of imagination, and that this imagination is written out in the treasuries of our kings and the gardens of our queens. Benjamin, who had a Third Imagination, could not 'contemplate without horror' the cultural treasures which descended into his hands: 'There is no document of civilization which is not at the same time a document of barbarism. And just as such a document is not free of barbarism, barbarism taints also the manner in which it was transmitted from one owner to another.'[3] This is the voice of a European person speaking to European peoples out of a Third Imagination. Benjamin's 'Theses on the Philosophy of History' deploy the rhetoric of the second world frequently, but in fact he lived an uneasy existence, at the margins of both of the first two worlds. For when he says that the task of the 'historical materialist' is 'to brush history against the grain'[4] he could not exclude the atrocious histories of the second world as well, where the violence of the first world has met its match.

What would it mean, then, to acquire a Third Imagination? On this question Fanon is clearer than Benjamin – even for European persons like ourselves. He sketches an answer (it is not written for us, but we can read it with profit) in his essay 'On National Culture'. According to Fanon, in the context of imperialism a national culture develops in three phases. (Fanon, of course, writes of these matters from the perspective of an actual citizen of the actual Third World; his analysis reflects on circumstances in the first two worlds as well, however, since the latter live through, by carrying out, the imagination of violence visited upon the Third World.) In the first phase of its development a cultural mode of violation is established and assimilated. In the second phase, when the violation is discovered, an effort is made to find a world elsewhere, an inviolate world: 'Past happenings of the byegone days of . . . childhood will be brought up out of the depths of . . . memory; old legends will be reinterpreted in the light of a borrowed estheticism and of a conception of the world which was discovered under other skies.'[5] This is a phase of enlightenment where the past is used to clarify conditions in the present. It prepares for the third phase, 'the fighting phase', when one 'turns himself into an awakener of the people', to 'shake' them from their lethargy.[6] The imagery echoes Fanon's call to a similar awakening of the 'European peoples' at the end of the essay 'Concerning Violence'.

In the third phase, past and present are conceived from the vantage of the future. In terms of an actual literary practice, the third phase means, for example, that 'The storytellers who used to relate inert episodes now bring them alive and introduce into them modifications which are increasingly fundamental.' 'Conflicts' are brought 'up to date and . . . modernize[d]', and 'The method of allusion is more and more widely used': 'The formula "This all happened long ago" is substituted with that of "What we are going to speak of happened somewhere else, but it might well have happened here today, and it might happen tomorrow."'[7] What Fanon means is that an imagination of the future, of what the future should be, determines both the writing and the reading of the texts we inherit and create. This third phase, which is one with the Third World, is the Third World's gift to 'the whole of mankind' – an objective and precisely an *alienated* perspective on the dialectic of violence of the first two worlds and all the 'inert episodes' which we fondly call our literary and cultural inheritance.

For the nations of the first and second worlds, with their imperialist histories, the awakening Fanon speaks of would expose new ranges of historical possibility – new configurations of the past, different imaginations of the present and the future. Our cultural productions generally represent those histories in forms of beauty and sublimity, though in fact they are histories which, as often as not, are founded in shameful and barbarous deeds. A critical awakening would strip away such modes of deception (and self-deception); it would entail a refusal to read our cultural deposits on their own ideological terms, and a refusal as well to develop new readings (or writings) that merely modernize and update those ideologies.

Initially this requires that our cultural works be alienated from the tradition that represents them as the best that has been known and thought in the world. This alienation does not mean, however, that the works should be debunked. Neither an antithetical nor a third reading can afford to deliver any part of cultural history into the hands of an imperial imagination. Rather, the works must be raised up from their narrowly imagined totalities, must be seen as part of that larger context that emerges when they are *specifically* situated, when they are delivered over to their historical and social localities. That critical event – the islanding of history and its works[8] – establishes the possibility of a proper sphere of totalization – one that is horizontally international, and vertically transcultural and transhistorical.

This islanding of the works of culture is especially crucial for readers in a Western tradition, where the intertexture of our cultural works, in particular of our poetry, has woven a net that is strangling human imagination. The burden of the past that weighs like a nightmare on the brain of the West is an imperial burden, the anxiety that it might not all be of one piece, that secret histories, forgotten facts, other imaginations operate in all that we do and make, and that our massive ignorance of these Othernesses is working to undermine what we do. Like Napoleon moving inexorably towards the capture of Moscow, Great Traditions follow their difficult and equivocal victories of imagination to an ultimate destruction.

That destruction does not overtake the works of the past, it merely makes them inaccessible to people in the present who are unable to imagine them anew, objectively. Writers like Benjamin and Fanon call us towards that objectivity, to an imagining of poetical work in ways that will be trying to overcome the illusions those works themselves have helped to perpetuate. Every poem is an island that imagines itself a world; and it *is* a world – but not *the* world – because it is a world within and among other worlds. Its illusion of totality is a dream of a truth that can only come to be in the exposure of the meaning of the dream.

A work like the *Oresteia*, for example, dreams of a society to be founded for ever in an imagination of justice and civil harmony. This utopian dream is then realized in Aeschylus' work, which we have since continued to interpret in terms that accommodate its own self-conception. Yet such interpretations visit a serious injustice upon the *Oresteia* and its utopian dream of a just and harmonious society. Justice here depends upon the exposition of the objective and alienated truths of Aeschylus' dramatic work. Such an exposition can never be completed, of course, but it will not even advance beyond a mirror-stage unless the work is seen objectively.

As we know, the *Oresteia* deals with the impasse which a retributive system of justice develops for itself. Or rather, it *imagines* such a system at an impasse – for in fact one could have imagined it otherwise, could have told a different story in which retribution falls upon the guilty by hands that are other than familial hands.

But Aeschylus wants to imagine retributive justice at an impasse because he wants to celebrate not simply a 'universal' idea of justice, but the Athenian version of a universal idea of justice. The play is presented in Athens at a crucial and specific time, 458 BC, shortly after the passage of the revolutionary Ephialtic reforms.[9] Scholars have long recognized this topical dimension to the *Oresteia*, and in more recent years have reached a certain broad agreement that Aeschylus, though generally conservative, must have supported a number of these new legal reforms. The trilogy makes a significant ideological intervention in the immediate aftermath of the struggle between the reformers (like Ephialtes and Pericles) and the traditional authorities (like Kimon).

The Ephialtic reforms were an attempt to replace the traditional oligarchic legal structure with democratic structures. As such, they were equally bound up with certain international issues, and most specifically with the uneasy relations (and alliance) between Sparta and Athens following the Persian Wars. Sparta, of course, was an oligarchy, and Athens' alliance with her was maintained and supported, at the crucial period of the reforms, largely through the authority of men like Kimon, who were sympathetic to oligarchic structures.

The context in which the reforms were passed is important if we are to understand the *Oresteia*.¹⁰ Athens had been asked to send a supporting force to Laconia to aid the Spartans in putting down the revolt of their helots in 463. Kimon argued successfully, against strong democratic opposition, to send an Athenian contingent, but when the army arrived in Laconia – with Kimon at its head – it was ignominiously sent away by the suspicious Lacedæmonians. Kimon returned to Athens in disgrace, the reforms were passed in 462/1 and Kimon was ostracized. But the reforms were not instituted without vigorous and widespread opposition, and great civic unrest in Athens. Ephialtes himself was assassinated shortly after the passage of the initial series of reforms.

The *Oresteia* is clearly preoccupied with all these matters; indeed, one of its principal objects, as we see most clearly at the end of *The Eumenides*, is to promote an ideal of civic harmony, and (reciprocally) to warn of the dangers that beset a society torn by internal and civil discord. At the end of *The Libation Bearers*, with Clytemnestra and Aegisthus now dead at the hands of the avenging Orestes, and with Orestes pursued by the Fates, the Chorus – dismayed at the prospect of a ceaseless process of internecine death – prays for an end to the bloodletting:

> Where
> Is the end? Where shall the fury of fate
> Be stilled to sleep, be done with?
> (1074–6)¹¹

The prayer recalls the refrain of the Chorus at the beginning of the *Agamemnon* ('Sing sorrow, sorrow: but good win out in the end'), and anticipates the conclusion of the trilogy, when the judgement of Athena – at the trial and immediately afterwards – produces the trilogy's final vision of civil harmony.

That vision is itself crucial to the resolution of the dramatic conflicts. After the acquittal of Orestes the Fates are at first implacable in their resentment, but Athena persuades them out of their wrath with benevolent promises. These are all founded in a conviction that Athens is destined for greatness:

> If you go away into some land of foreigners,
> I warn you, you will come to love this country. Time

in his forward flood shall ever grow more dignified
for the people of this city. And you, in your place
of eminence beside Erechtheus in his house
shall win from female and from male processionals
more than all lands of men beside could ever give.
(851–7)

This is a social and a political vision, and it celebrates what the final courtroom scene dramatizes: Aeschylus' conviction that the institutions of Athens are the glory of Greece – indeed, the glory of the world. Important to the meaning of the conclusion of *The Eumenides* is the fact that a stranger to Athens, a guest, should go there to seek justice. Athens took a justifiable pride in her legal institutions, and specifically in the two fundamental principles: that rule should be maintained by law and not by men, and that everyone – guest and citizen alike – should have equal protection under the law. The conclusion of *The Eumenides* is a celebration of those legal institutions.

But the play is also celebrating something else – a treaty of alliance with Argos made in 461 at the urging of the (now politically dominant) reform party. This second focus of celebration is closely allied to the first. It is a celebration not of Athens' political institutions, however, but of her economic and political power. The two celebrations are connected in the reality of Athens' circumstances in the period 463–458, when Athens arrived at a position of enormous economic, military and political power and influence. This position was achieved gradually during the period following the Persian Wars, but most dramatically between 477 and 463, that is, between the founding of the Delian League – with Athens at its head – and the subjugation by Athens of various members who tried to revolt from the League. The important island of Thasos was reduced in 463 after a two-year struggle. During the fifteen-year period between the foundation of the League and the Ephialtic reforms, Athens' empire came into being.

These matters bear upon the *Oresteia* because the treaty with Argos is the play's device for focusing our attention on Athens' position in the Greek world at the time. Aeschylus draws our attention to Argos immediately, at the opening of the *Agamemnon* (24), when we are told that the king is returning home from the

Trojan War to Argos. According to Homer, however, Agamemnon was the king of Mykenai, not of Argos. Scholars agree now that this change was made as a compliment to Athens' new ally.[12] The change was not an awkward one in any case since the Argives had recently conquered the ancient city of Mykenai and incorporated her into their domains.[13]

The conquest of Mykenai was the latest in a series of adventures that placed Argos in a position to rival Sparta for control of the Peloponnese. Athens sought the treaty with Argos – a defensive alliance against Sparta – immediately after the failure of Kimon's expedition into Laconia to aid Sparta. The alliance with Argos, in other words, was an international part of the democratic reforms being carried through by Ephialtes and Pericles. The alliance was meant to strengthen the Athenian Empire against its chief rival for power in Greece, Sparta.

Aeschylus alludes to this treaty with Argos three times in *The Eumenides* and in each case the passage imagines an alliance 'for the rest of time' (291, 670). In the final passage Orestes, speaking as the mouthpiece of Argos, swears to fight with Athens against those who come against her, and to be the 'gracious spirit' of all those others, her tributaries and her allies, who 'align their spears to fight beside her' (773–4). Orestes' oath of alliance is immediately followed by the scene in which Athena finally persuades the Furies to take up their office of benevolence towards Athens. Before the play concludes in its vision of civic harmony, Athena addresses the as yet unpersuaded Furies. 'Do not', she warns them,

> engraft among my citizens that spirit of war
> that turns their battle fury inward on themselves.
> No, let our wars range outward . . .
>
> (862–4)

The prayer expresses at once Aeschylus' dismay at the recent civil discords in Athens between the rival democratic and aristocratic parties, and his confidence in the martial strength of the empire in face of her enemies. The confidence here is part of the trilogy's compliment to Argos, whose alliance added so much to Athenian imperial power vis-à-vis the other Greek cities, and especially the Lacedæmonians.

Yet hidden in the splendour of the play's conclusion, with its grandiose imagination of social harmony, is a terrible truth which the ideology of Aeschylus' trilogy could not see, but which the dramas are none the less forced to confront. For the fact is that this very alliance with Argos, which seemed to promise so much good, was the triggering event behind the (so-called) 'First' Peloponnesian War, and the first act in a tragic curve that would eventually plunge all of Greece into war and bring about the destruction of the empire so vaunted in the *Oresteia*. Athena, goddess though she is, cannot understand the full, tragic weight of her prayer for outward-ranging war. In its imagination of an end to the cycles of bloodshed, the *Oresteia* is prophesying an even greater cataclysm, and no end to the cycles of destruction. For the *Oresteia*'s imagination of justice and harmony are illusions, founded in a set of contradictory social structures (democracy and imperialism) which would only grow more extreme with the passing of time.

We do not understand how poetry works if we think that, because the Peloponnesian Wars took place after Aeschylus wrote the *Oresteia*, therefore the trilogy and those wars are not implicated in each other. We may imagine, rather, that the 'meaning' of a poetical work is structured by the historical limit of the author's life; and this imagining is all the more insisted upon when the 'meanings' we seek after are social and historical ones. But we are wrong in this imagining, because every poetical work casts itself along what Shelley called 'futurity'. In writing what amounts to an imaginative history of the present, poems thereby construct a past and a set of possible futures. One of the futures constructed in the *Oresteia* is 'an upright course clear through to the end' (995) and 'peace forever' (1046). But another future, more dreadful, is also constructed through the play *in the very illusions and contradictions that are borne along with that first, benevolent imagination of the future*. The tragic meaning of the *Oresteia* is not a mere quirk or irony of history; it is what the trilogy signified from the beginning, and what was most dramatically foregrounded in the celebrations of the treaty with Argos.

Poems move out into many futures, which are their own real futures as well, unknown to themselves. The *Oresteia* today means both more and less than it meant in 458 because its meaning — which is always localized in the present — carries along the many histories of meanings that were only initiated in the trilogy's first appearance. These meanings are sometimes lost, often recovered and always refashioned. If we read the *Oresteia*'s conclusion as an unequivocal celebration we will be reading it in terms of its initial self-conception; and we will be reading *out* of the work that other dominant line of meaning which is so closely connected to the celebratory meaning, and which is so intimately involved with the work's history – with the work as meaning in and through the history its own celebration calls our attention to.

We will, moreover, be reading in a way that projects a certain meaning into our own immediate circumstances. More clearly than most works of the past, the *Oresteia* seems to impinge upon ourselves and our present. This work and its significant history 'all happened long ago', but Fanon's suggestion – that 'it might well have happened here today, and it might happen tomorrow' – points towards the 'formula' that all criticism, whether consciously or not, adheres to. The tales told in the *Oresteia* are certainly happening here today, and will happen again tomorrow. The question is: how will we choose to read those tales – objectively, or in terms of their own (and our own) celebrations and self-conceptions?

Shelley wrote the *Prometheus Unbound* as a response to the future bequeathed to him by Aeschylus' *Prometheus Bound* and the (subsequently lost) *Prometheus Unbound*, with its celebratory reconciliation of 'the Champion with the Oppressor of mankind'.[14] Shelley's play is a reading of the lost Aeschylean drama according to Fanon's 'method of allusion' and 'modernization': not an imitation, but a remaking in terms of a more objective imagining of Aeschylus than the Greek dramatist would have intended. Aeschylean drama, however, like all poetry, lays down a rich deposit of incommensurate detail even as it follows its specific ideological commitments. In this way poetry always tells more than it knows, always carries within itself many opportunities for greater objectivity and truth.

Genesis, more than most texts, has worked assiduously to project a monomorphic image of its world; but even in Genesis the relics of a larger story remain, a story that includes many other cultures and civilizations as great, and as barbaric, as Israel's. The Israel of Genesis is an island in a greater world, and the more it insists that it is the centre of that world, the more it gives us glimpses of the actual, the whole, the objective truth.

To relinquish an empire is no easy task, and it can be, as Pericles once argued, dangerous as well.[15] To maintain one, however, is not merely wrong – which Pericles observed – it is even more dangerous. The dangers are especially acute in the case of empires like the Athenian and the American – empires, that is to say, that were acquired in a brief period and only half-purposefully, empires that developed in volatile political circumstances both at home and abroad.

To relinquish an imperial imagination is also a difficult if no less urgent task. Empires are maintained by imperial intellects. Cultural studies, and literary work in particular, function either to build or to unbuild such minds. In this respect Blake's work is exactly a prophecy against empire, a model of how the poetic moves against the perpetuation of empires and towards the development of less exploitive societies, less alienated imaginations. Literary work is the art of multiplicities and minute particulars, the science of *Un*buildings: One law for the lion and the ox *is* oppression.

In this context Shelley's famous words bear remembering:

> We have more moral, political and historical wisdom, than we know how to reduce to practise; we have more scientific and economical knowledge than can be accommodated to the just distribution of the produce which it multiplies ... our calculations have outrun conception; we have eaten more than we can digest. The cultivation of those sciences which have enlarged the limits of the empire of man over the external world, has, for want of the poetical faculty, proportionately circumscribed those of the internal world; and man, having enslaved the elements, remains himself a slave.[16]

These are stirring words, and worthy of honour – not least because they are fully conscious that poetical work is not an aesthetic resort but an activity with real social investments and obligations. They are as well, however, words spoken out of that fundamental Romantic Ideology which is epitomized in the Kantian aesthetic, but which is equally operative in the anti-Kantian Romantic programme first deployed by Blake. That is to say, Shelley – like Blake before him – takes it for granted that the redemption of the social order is the function of the 'poetical faculty'. For them, poetry and Imagination are not involved with the false consciousness of ideology.

Yet it is plain that this ascription of transcendent status to art and the Imagination is mistaken – indeed, is contradicted by the actual practice of Romantic artists themselves. Milton earlier established the model that, in place of a failed social order, one might establish the order of an inward paradise. But neither Blake nor Shelley – nor even Wordsworth, for that matter – accepted Milton's consolatory move. Their departures from Milton's model all differ somewhat, of course, but Blake's departure is especially significant because his work enacts an artistic practice that is committed to the transformation of society: the installation of the city of God (which for Blake means a *human* city) in England's green and pleasant land.

Blake understands that this will be a city of art, that is to say, a city in which all the work will be artists' work – work designed to move against (though it will never entirely defeat) what Shelley called 'Fate, Time, Occasion, Chance, and Change'. It will be a social order with no 'corporeal war', an order entirely cleansed of 'the Wastes of moral law'. None of these imaginations are 'inward' imaginations; they are emphatically political, institutional, even economic – as Blake's prose works repeatedly emphasize.

Blake's work is important, in this context, because it consistently foregrounds the material, social and institutional bases of its productive modes. Unlike Shelley and the other Romantics, he took none of art's productive processes and institutions for granted. An imaginative and poetical transformation of the social order is carried out at all levels and in every form of that order. His illuminated poems are especially clear examples of his understanding that if art is to be an agent of change, its agencies will be operating at the earliest stages of conception and through all later productive, distributive and reproductive phases. None of this must be allowed to escape poetry's concrete transformative deliberations.

If Blake's judgements about these matters went far beyond the other artists of his time – and I think they did – the irony is that he became, none the less, the most ineffectual of that period's many angels. No one had less influence on his age than Blake, and it would be many decades after his death before he would begin to gather a public arena. And now he is an academic subject, central to the curriculum.

It was not what he had in mind. In *The Marriage of Heaven and Hell* 'the cherub with his flaming sword' – that is to say, the angel of the social apocalypse – '*is* hereby commanded to leave his guard at tree of life' (plate 14; my italics). But the angel of history did not appear to obey that poetic command, which Blake gave in this early poem and which he repeated in all his works throughout his career. (In fact, the command was obeyed as it was issued, only its accomplishment came in forms of truth which Blake had not thought of.) As with Aeschylus in *The Eumenides*, the future of Blake's work would bear along with that work, and for that work, as much history as it had imagined, but far more than it knew.

Are they fortuitous, these discordant artistic futures, and irrelevant to the ways we should understand and use our poetic resources? I do not think so. When we think of poems 'in their historical contexts', our historicist biases – even in their 'New Historicist' modes – take those 'contexts' to be located primarily in the past, or – if we have read our Nietzsche and Foucault with care – in the present and the past. And when we think even more deeply about such matters we also understand that these historical contexts are multiple and conflicting: heteroglossial, as Bakhtin would say. But if it is true that all futures are functions of the past (and the present), then we must expect to find those futures being carried out in the works that seem to be speaking and acting only from the past.

Poems imagine more than they know. The *Oresteia* is a far greater work, in those future contexts of reality it had not discussed and did not desire, than it is when we read it merely in the context of its own grandiose – and mistaken – self-conceptions. Its greatness is intimately bound up with its own imaginative capacities, which solicit the total appearance of the human truth of things – that is to say, their social and historical truth, in all its contradictions and emergencies. And the same is true for Blake's work, which, like the *Oresteia*, looked forward to the advent of a New Jerusalem. But it did not come. The violent would bear it away, and Blake would play his part in the closet dramas of the academy and the struggles in the auction salesrooms.

Blake's distinctly non-radical reception history is an irony very like the one we saw in the future of the *Oresteia*; the irony is no more an aberration for Blake's work, however, than it was for Aeschylus'. There are more things in Blake's heavens and hells than he thought of in his philosophy. Though his mode of artistic production involved a conscious effort to avoid the machineries of mercantile capitalism, it also ensured that his work would be expensive, even in his own day. The provenance histories of the illuminated works show that they have, with few exceptions, been sought after and owned by rich people and art connoisseurs.[17] Thus, although Blake's ideas and goals looked to the material transformation of unjust and exploitive social conditions, the 'vehicular forms' of these projects had, from the outset, small purchase among those who would be most interested in carrying out such social transformations. Unlike Shelley and Byron, for example, Blake was unknown to the Chartists. He was delivered into the aesthetic hands of the Pre-Raphaelites through quietist religious agencies: that is to say, through that pious circle of men who called themselves the 'Ancients' and Blake the 'Interpreter' – men like John Linnell, George Cumberland, Frederick Tatham, George Richmond and of course Alexander Gilchrist.[18] Similarly, though we can see that, in Blake's day, the New Jerusalem Church and other dissenting sects drew their strength from the underprivileged, the character of religious non-conformity had changed drastically between 1790 and 1830. The Evangelical Movement, in the first two decades of the nineteenth century, moved closer to the ideological mainstream of English society – so much so, in fact, that it had become an important reforming movement even within the Church of England by 1820.[19] We should not be surprised, therefore, that Blake would ask to have the Anglican service read at his funeral in 1827. It may seem an odd turn of events in the career of this great antinomian figure, but he was first and last a Christian, and his own work remained open – as it still remains open – to those clerical interpretations which survive in the valley of their saying, which make nothing happen beyond what has been established as possible or acceptable.

Once again, however, this is a historical eventuality that lies hidden within Blake's own work. That his ideas and goals were partly mystified in themselves seems quite clear, and not simply from his sexist theory of the emanations,[20] or his decision to write in such a way that the figure of a privileged 'Interpreter' would become so central to that correspondent breeze known as 'Blake Studies'. Even more crucial to the historical meaning of Blake's work was his conviction, which he shared with every major poet of his age, that art is a non-ideological agency. Of course Blake understood very well that imagination and poetry are human acts embedded in their times of conflicting vision and contested human interests. But he also – and contradictorily – believed that there could be – had to be – an originary Prophet of such Losses who would not be subject to those losses. A New Day would dawn with the Dawning of the Imagination, when the unfallen Zoa – Los, the Zoa of Poetic Creation – would assume an empire over the world. This idea – the Romantic Ideology of the Poet as Genius – is one of the last infirmities of those noble Romantic minds.

It was, in addition, a mental infirmity which they themselves recognized – in others. The Romantic 'interpretation' of Milton – vulgarly, that Satan is the hero of *Paradise Lost* – is not something which, in their view, had been laid upon Milton's work anachronistically. Blake's *Milton* argued the case against the great Puritan on the basis of English history, and especially the history of English imperial interests as they developed between Milton's day, on the one hand, and Blake's during the Napoleonic Wars, on the other. Blake's argument is that Milton's works contributed largely to the construction of that evil history; indeed, the famous 'paradise within', which Milton preached, is revealed in Blake's revisionary poem as the 'cold bosom' and corrupted heart of 'Albion', who sleeps in righteousness on his 'Rock of Ages'.

> The Nations still
> Follow after the detestable Gods of Priam; in pomp
> Of warlike selfhood, contradicting and blaspheming . . .
> I will go down to the sepulcher to see if morning breaks!
> I will go down to self-annihilation and eternal death,
> Lest the Last Judgement come & find me unannihilate
> And I be siez'd & giv'n into the hands of my own Selfhood.
> (14: 14–16, 20–4)

Milton's work constructs an image of the paradisal and the elect through a reciprocal definition of the hellish and the damned. It is an image founded, therefore, quite literally, in sin. Its consequence is an imperial history which, in political terms, reappeared in Blake's day as a dynamic of the Elect (England), the Reprobate (France) and the Redeemable (that which remains, the Third World). In such a scheme that Third World is to be appropriated to the missionary zeal of an Elected design. But to Blake such a design is not merely moral righteousness, it is actual political imperialism. To Blake it is a design founded in England, reinstituted in Milton and thence dispersed across the world in a process of real historical events.

>   Lambeth's Vale
> Where Jerusalems foundations began: where they were laid in ruins
> Where they were laid in ruins from every Nation
>   & Oak Groves rooted . . .
> When shall Jerusalem return & overspread all the Nations
> Return: return to Lambeths Vale O building of human souls
> Thence stony Druid Temples overspread the Island white
> And thence from Jerusalems ruins, from her walls of salvation
> And praise: thro the whole Earth were reard from Ireland
> To Mexico & Peru west, & east to China & Japan: till Babel
> The Spectre of Albion frownd over the Nations
>   in glory and war
> All things begin & end in Albions ancient Druid rocky shore.
>   (4: 14–16, 18–25)

England's spectrous presence is called Babel, in the context of these historical references, because she works to build an imperial city and to sacrifice all other cities to that monomorphic empire. From the ruins of Jerusalem – a plural reality, as we know from the conclusion of Blake's last major prophecy – emerges Babel, the great figure of all the Buildings of Loss. Its more common name is the British Empire.

Blake deployed a poetical scheme for imagining all the buildings of loss as the Buildings of Los: as the city of art, 'great Golgonooza', a place that opened out to the world of eternity. And eternity, Blake's ultimate object in several senses, stood apart from history and time and space because it incorporated, like a Hegelian dialectic, all of human history within itself. But *in truth* the Hegelian dialectic and Blake's 'Eternity' are, like Kant's aesthetic, historical formations; and their historicity is revealed most dramatically when they enter the fullness of time, that is, when Blake's 'Eternity' – or Hegel's dialectic, or Kant's aesthetic – are viewed in the perspective of a total form of history, which means that they are viewed in the perspective of a more encompassing – a more objective – form of history. That is the perspective of the unknown and the possible, the perspective which alone reveals the multiple histories that lie hidden, and as often as not repressed, within the works where they have been imagined, but where they are not recognized. These futures, which may be either terrible or wonderful, are the instruments through which all of history, past, present and future alike, is opened to change. Such an opening is what Blake supplied for Milton and his other cultural forebears. But while in this respect Blake, like Jesus, saved those others, of himself we have to think – it is one of the few (terrible) insights left to an imperialist imagination – that 'himself he could not save'. He could not, quite simply, because he had held back – because he had 'saved' – a part of his work that was to be placed for ever beyond the possibility of either fall or redemption.

In fact, there is nothing that can be set apart in that way; and the idea that Eternity exists outside of its various human imaginations (of which Blake's is only one) is an immortalist illusion. In Romantic art it reappears as the idea of the aesthetic, and while Blake fought against that idea, his own work ultimately submitted to its domination. Its illusory character, so far as poetic work is concerned, would not be fully and consciously re-exposed until the twentieth century, in the unfolding of Ezra Pound's great poetical project the *Cantos*. (I say *(re-)exposed* because the transcendentalizing of poetry and imaginative agencies is by no means characteristic of the cultural periods of the West – even the Christian West – before the coming of Romanticism.)

Had Byron begun writing *Don Juan* when he began *Childe Harold's Pilgrimage* in 1809, and had he gone on with it all his life and lived until (let us say) 1870 or so, he might have produced something comparable to the *Cantos*. I sketch this literary fantasy because it calls attention to certain important similarities, and even more important differences, between *Don Juan*, and Pound's epic. In the first place, both works are produced in a seriatim process. *Don Juan* is published in six separate parts over a five-year period, and the separate volumes reflect that passage of time and its circumstantialities. The work replicates, in this respect, the serial publication of *Childe Harold's Pilgrimage*, which was issued in three separate volumes between 1812 and 1818, and which was written over a ten-year period. Byron's work refuses to proceed upon 'system'; the horizon of *Don Juan*'s expectations is close and short, and the poem cultivates, as we know, a series of immediacies. 'Note or text, / I never know the word which will come next' (*Don Juan* IX st. 41). With this deliberate cultivation of inconsequence (the word should be taken in several senses) Byron defies the highest poetical canons of his age, most especially those of Kant, Coleridge and Hegel. As he got further along with *Don Juan* he began to imagine a conclusion – the death of Juan on the guillotine in the Reign of Terror – and he seems to have begun to prepare for that event.[21] But in the work that we have, the seriatim process persists to the end.

Unlike Byron, Pound began the *Cantos* with definite plans and preconceptions, nor did he put into question the Romantic criterion of Total Form. On the contrary, in setting out to write a *Commedia* appropriate to his epoch, Pound's plan was fairly dominated by the idea of Total Form. The idea captured him because, even more than the writers and poets of 1780–1830, Pound confronted an epoch – particularly from 1914, the year before he began the *Cantos* – that surpassed even Byron's age in its cultural fragmentation and social barbarity. 'These fragments you have shelved (shored)' (VIII. 1): that theme directs the *Cantos* from the first. But Pound's initial articulation works some telling puns on the words 'shelved' and 'shored': in addition to their obvious primary meanings, both words suggest 'fragments' that have come or been washed ashore, like Odysseus at Phaiakia or his other stopping places.

Pound's method for negotiating that treacherous world was what he called the periplum, or what he understood as point-by-point navigation. That method of proceeding is the equivalent of Byron's seriatim manoeuvres, only in Pound's case it is initiated in concert with a quest for Total Form (social as well as aesthetic, it should be understood). As it turned out, the production history of the *Cantos* became a kind of periplum in time. Ten separate 'books' of the work are printed from 1925 to 1969, and individual Cantos or parts of Cantos – some later revised or rejected altogether – were published in various magazines and journals. The first pieces of the poem appear in print in 1915, and to this day – Pound died in 1972 – further unpublished fragments continue to appear.[22]

It has been wittily (and justly) said that 'The eleven Pisan Cantos were written at a time [1945] when the poem including history found itself included in history.'[23] In truth, however, the *Cantos* were *always* 'included in history', as the production history of the poem emphasizes. The Pisan Cantos are special only because they dramatize that inclusion beyond any possibility of mistake or unawareness. For more than fifty years – 1915 to 1969 – the *Cantos* moved through the twentieth century, appearing at intervals to reflect the European/American mind back to itself. The effort was to bring (or restore) coherence to that mind. In the end – in the great tragic texts of *Drafts and Fragments* of 1969, a malebolge year of this century's Western and imperialist wars – Pound echoed Byron's 'Epistle to Augusta':[24]

> Tho' my errors and wrecks lie about me.
> And I am not a demigod,
> I cannot make it cohere.
>
> (CXVI)

'I lost my center / fighting the world', he remarks in the 'Notes for CXVII et seq.'; for in this quest after a 'paradiso/terrestre', Pound discovers that what initially appeared as fragmentation and contradiction was precisely that: 'The dreams clash / and are shattered.'

The greatness of the *Cantos* is in large part a function of its chronology, and its involvement in the real history that is schematized in that chronology. The poem begins with the goal of Total Form as it had been framed and imperially imagined in the West between 1780 and 1915. The poem then tests that imagination as it continues to reimagine itself, more brutally than it ever did in the nineteenth century, from the First World War to Vietnam. The great *artistic* benefit to a work that has been produced over such a long period is that time and circumstances – if the poem is honest with itself – will play havoc with its most cherished illusions. In the *Cantos* we finally see, fully displayed, the brutal truth of the Western dialectic as Benjamin had framed it: 'There is no document of civilization which is not at the same time a document of barbarism.'

Of course, when the academy reads such a poem it has ways of avoiding its imaginations. One way is to celebrate the *Cantos* for its 'beauties', for its local achievements and its grand aspirations. These things are accepted. Reciprocally, the poem will have its horrors denounced, deplored or set aside: its antisemitism and racism, for example, or its unrepentant adherence to fascist programmes. If one takes this way with the poem, all these matters are accepted at face value, as if the beauties were evidently beauties and the horrors, horrors, as if they were all understandable to persons of sympathy and taste.

Another way is more critical. It will argue that somehow the beauties and the horrors are functions of each other, that the former will only have been gained – in so far as they *are* gained – through a concert with the latter. In this view the poem is internally self-contradicted, and is to be read as a moral exemplum or cautionary tale.[25]

But in truth neither this poem, nor any other poem or cultural product, ought to be read from such a safe – such an imperial – distance. Not in the West, at any rate. The distanced reader is what Baudelaire knew to be a hypocritical reader. Pound's exposure of European and American imperialism loses none of its *objective* truth because it comes from a source which is in so many ways repellent and blind. To Pound it was a complex centred in England, a complex from which Germany and Italy sought to free themselves. But increasingly we can see that that complex is a parodic god whose centre is everywhere and whose circumference is nowhere. The European wars of this century were mugs' games – like Russia, France and England struggling with the Ottoman Empire at the end of the eighteenth century for control of Greece and the east Mediterranean trade routes. If Pound excepted Mussolini's Italy from the twentieth century's Western ways – if he excepted himself, and if he sought to represent his exceptional condition in the *Cantos* – we may think or say that he failed. But the more important thought is that the *Cantos* finally imagined the failure they did not know – imagined it throughout, as a total form, though that imaginative form only began to raise the failure into a form of consciousness in the last twenty-five years of the work's production.

During those years – 1945 to 1969 – the academy began its

quest to 'understand' the *Cantos*, and to this day it has produced those two ways of reading the poem I have mentioned. Yet they will not do. The poem does not permit a distanced reading, and in this respect it carries out a definitive break with the Romantic ideology of immanent form (the Kantian 'aesthetic'). Immanent, 'readerly' criticism, the last serious bastion of this Kantian norm, re-established aesthetic space in the reader after Modernism in art began the labour to dis-establish it from the work.

The *Cantos* is important, therefore, because – as a poem evidently included in history – it has explained once again, more clearly than at any time since the eighteenth century, that all poems and cultural products are included in history – *including* the producers and the reproducers of such works, the poets and their readers and interpreters. But the *Cantos* is even more significant for its revelation of the meaning of history. To the historicist imagination, history is the past, or perhaps the past as seen in and through the present; and the historical task is to attempt a reconstruction of the past, including, perhaps, the present of that past. But the *Cantos* reminds us that history includes the future, and that the historical task involves as well the construction of what shall be possible. Delivered through the world over such a long and momentous period of time, the *Cantos* managed to gather into itself, and then foreground, parts of its own futurity. History in this poem thereby revealed itself as the fullness of time – a fullness whose shape(s) and direction(s) will never be completely known, though they will always be anticipated.

Poetical work, Aristotle said, is more philosophical than history. If this is so then it is also more 'historical' than history, as Nietzsche argued, because the 'history' that poems touch and re-present encompasses a far greater scale of possible, and therefore real, human times and events than the most careful and scholarly historical text. Indeed, the greatest of such texts – Herodotus, the Bible, Thucydides – have set themselves apart by actively embracing different types of imaginative procedures. Poetical works are historically overdetermined – littered with incommensurate materials that grow only more multiple when they are delivered over to further readings and uses. What they do not know – which is a great deal, the abyss of their ignorance – they will have imagined. The *Oresteia* and the *Cantos* are unusual only because they have so graphically displayed this fault line – ultimately catastrophic – of their non-consciousness; in this respect they epitomize the resources of all poetical discourse, whose knowledge is heterological.

When we read we construct our histories, including our futures. In our day, this peculiar Western moment, poetry's special contribution to that process – poetry's special form of 'reading' – comes as a set of complicating and undermining procedures. Calling into question all that is privileged, understood and given, including itself, this poetry operates under the signs of Difference and, most especially, of Change. And this poetry has thereby set us our models for reading the works that descend to us from 'tradition'. What is astonishing here is the way our literary inheritance seems to have anticipated these contemporary uses – seems, as it were, to have intended them.

Notes

1 Frantz Fanon, *The Wretched of the Earth*, Preface by Jean-Paul Sartre, trans. Constance Farrington (New York: Grove Press, 1968), p. 105.
2 Ibid., p. 106.
3 Walter Benjamin, *Illuminations*, ed. Hannah Arendt, trans. Harry Zohn (New York: Schocker Books, 1969), p. 256.
4 Ibid., p. 257.
5 Fanon, *The Wretched of the Earth*, p. 222.
6 Ibid., pp. 222-3.
7 Ibid., p. 240.
8 I mean to recall here Marshall Sahlins's *Islands of History* (Chicago: University of Chicago Press, 1985), and in general the book's important demonstration of how an imperial culture encounters, and mistakes, the histories in which it is involved.
9 The best single presentation of the historical and political context of the *Oresteia* is in Anthony J. Podlecki's *The Political Background of Aeschylean Tragedy* (Ann Arbor: University of Michigan Press, 1966), ch. 5.
10 See George Grote, *A History of Greece* (New York: Hasper, 1881) vol. II, chs 45-6.
11 I use here Richard Lattimore's translation (Chicago: University of Chicago Press, 1953).
12 See e.g. James C. Hogan, *A Commentary on The Complete Greek Tragedies. Aeschylus* (Chicago: University of Chicago Press, 1984), pp. 31, 159-60.
13 See Grote, *A History of Greece*, p. 411.

14 From Shelley's Preface to *Prometheus Unbound*, in *Shelley's Poetry and Prose*, ed. Donald H. Reiman and Sharon B. Powers (New York: Norton, 1977), p. 133.
15 See Thucydides, *The Peloponnesian War*, Book II, sec. 63.
16 From Shelley's 'Defence of Poetry', *Shelley's Poetry and Prose*, pp. 502–3.
17 For information on the provenance histories of Blake's works see Gerald Bentley, Jr, *Blake Books* (Oxford: Oxford University Press, 1977).
18 See Gerald Bentley, Jr, *Blake Records* (Oxford: Oxford University Press, 1969). My Blake texts here are quoted from *The Poetry and Prose of William Blake*, newly revised edition by David V. Erdman, with a commentary by Harold Bloom (Berkeley: University of California Press, 1982).
19 See Kenneth Scott Latourette, *A History of Christianity in the 19th and 20th Centuries*, vol. II (Grand Rapids, Mich.: Zondervan, 1969), chs 16–19.
20 See Anne K. Mellor, 'Blake's Portrayal of Women', *Blake/ An Illustrated Quarterly*, vol. 16 (Winter 1982–3), pp. 148–65.
21 For Byron's plans to have Juan executed in the Reign of Terror see *Byron. The Poetical Works*, ed. Jerome J. McGann (Oxford: Oxford University Press, 1986), vol. V, p. xxiii.
22 For the bibliographical history of the *Cantos* see Donald Gallup, *Ezra Pound, a Bibliography* (Charlottesville: University Press of Virginia, 1983). A good discussion of the bibliography can be found in Alan Durant, *Ezra Pound: Identity in Crisis* (Hassocks, Sussex: Harvester, 1981), ch. 3.
23 George Kearns, *Guide to Ezra Pound's Selected Cantos* (New Brunswick, NJ: Rutgers University Press, 1980), p. 149.
24 For the Byron text Pound is recalling see *Byron. The Poetical Works*, ed. McGann, vol.IV, pp. 33–5 ('Stanzas to [Augusta]').
25 The second is the way Michael Bernstein has proceeded in his excellent *The Tale of the Tribe. Ezra Pound and the Modern Verse Epic* (Princeton, NJ: Princeton University Press, 1980). His book is at the same time a conscious critique of all readings of the *Cantos* that operate as if the poem were transparent to itself.

4

Keats and Critique

Paul Hamilton

> The beautiful forms displayed in the organic world all plead eloquently on the side of the realism of the aesthetic finality of nature in support of the plausible assumption that beneath the production of the beautiful there must lie a preconceived idea in the producing cause – that is to say an *end* acting in the interest of our imagination.
>
> Kant, Critique of Judgement, ¶58

> In this relation [of Romantic art] the inner, so pushed to the extreme, is an expression without any externality at all; it is invisible and is as it were a perception of itself alone, or a musical sound as such without objectivity and shape, or a hovering over the waters, or a ringing tone over a world which in and on its heterogeneous phenomena can only accept and re-mirror a reflection of the inwardness of soul.
>
> Hegel, Aesthetics, 527

I

In a letter of 16 August 1820, Keats wrote to Shelley:

> A modern work it is said must have a purpose, which may be the God – *an artist* must serve Mammon – he must have 'self-concentration' selfishness perhaps. You I am sure will forgive me for sincerely remarking that you might curb your magnanimity and be more of an artist, and 'load every rift' of your subject with ore. The thought of such discipline must fall like cold chains upon you, who perhaps never sat with your wings furl'd for six months together, And is this not extraordina[r]y talk for the writer of Endymion?

whose mind was like a pack of scattered cards – I am pick'd up and sorted to a pip. My Imagination is a Monastry and I am its Monk – you must explain my metap^{cs} [metaphysics] to yourself.

Keats's readers inherit a critical tradition in which his own language is regarded as being everywhere as loaded and mixed in its blessings as that recommended here to Shelley. His 'metap^{cs} [metaphysics]', as he told Shelley in the same letter, 'you must explain . . . to yourself' (II, 323). In a recent issue of *Studies in Romanticism* providing a forum for the subject of 'Keats and Politics', the editor, Susan Wolfson, mentions a 'general critical tendency to regard the very conjunction of "Keats" and "politics" as something of a metaphysical conceit'.[1] Yet when Keats asks Shelley to curb his presumably political 'magnanimity' in the interests of being 'more of an artist', he characterizes this aestheticism as devotion to 'Mammon' rather than to 'God', paradoxically (so it seems) recalling the material interests of politics through his very appeal to artistic idealism. By shifting the accents in that unexpected verbal conjunction, we realize that Keats's metaphysics, or his writerly situation *within* rather than reference *to* a current metaphysical configuration, has been ignored as much as his politics. In working them out 'for yourself', 'you' find that the aura of 'metaphysical conceit' apparently unrealizing Keats's politics is the clue to their nature.

This is one of the pioneering insights of Marjorie Levinson's book, *Keats's Life of Allegory – the Origins of a Style*. At last one can see clearly the conceitfulness with which Keats's poems double and displace their political concerns. Furthermore, we learn to read these concerns not as something under Keats's conscious control, but as part of an exercise in 'doing to himself what others do to him'. At the same time, Levinson's work discovers in the prescribed perversity that this social effect reveals, the absence of that collective life which would, conventionally, explain the unfreedom of Keats's self-fashioning. Keats suffers the 'scandal of a man without a class', the 'neither–nor' of someone stationed between the lower and middling orders. In a doubly effacing movement, then, the Keatsian poet is subjected to a social determination which stems from an indeterminate social provenance. Moreover, Levinson shows that the bourgeois culture to which Keats aspires shares his uncertainty of origin and recognizes its prototype in him. *His* visibly disadvantaged perspective on bourgeois aesthetics thus accentuates *its* characteristic nothingness in a subversive parody, betraying its poverty, as Hyperion does the misery of the Titans, 'To the most hateful seeing of itself'. Levinson's interest in developing a sociology of Keatsian literariness requires a de-emphasis of the familiar semantic questions: 'Keats's 'solutions *do* solve metaphysical and epistemological problems, but it is the others that need explaining.'[2]

My own return to 'metaphysical and epistemological problems' tries to capitalize on the new visibility which the old problems have gained as a result of Levinson's study. Re-immersion in these problems may weaken the sense of Keatsian parody, but, as Levinson asserts, metaphysical problems *are* solved in Keats's writings; and an analysis like mine, which shows the poverty of these successes, may help us see what happened to the idealist aesthetic when submitted to those pressures which Levinson's cultural materialism has identified. To work within the scheme of Romantic idealism in relation to Keats is not, then, to forgo critique. It is, rather, to explore from within a frustrated and inhibited critique which is transformed into effective parody as soon as its strict immanence is abandoned. Thus do we start to explain the mutual displacement of the political and the metaphysical within the discursive economy of Keats's time. We consider the means by which Keats and his early critics hid from themselves the substantive issues cultural materialism reveals. Finally, we relate the subversive implausibility of this containment, a weakness sensed but of necessity protected by Keats's contemporaries, to the productive and absorptive aporiae of the Kantian aesthetic.

The 'metaphysical conceit' of Keats's politics is a way to name the manner in which two discourses reciprocally disguise each other. The fact that Keats's metaphysical is political and his political metaphysical makes each invisible and accounts for the proverbial absence of both from his work. The word for this common vanishing-point is the 'aesthetic'. In the Kantian tradition, the aesthetic is what is left of reality after the critical philosophy has performed its task. A critique which, like Keats's poetry, operates under the sign of the aesthetic might therefore be expected to remain fairly well hidden. The aesthetic is also the area in which politics consolidates itself as culture; in which, again in line with

Kantian practice, universals are imaginatively negotiated rather than deduced, and the political character of such transactions is both masked and validated as the exposition of what is metaphysically possible.[3]

My argument is that the interchangeability in Keats's poetry of its ideal status and its political reticence gradually begins to expose the contemporary politicizing of the ideal and the idealizing of the political. Moreover, in speaking that aesthetic function, the poetry breaks the silence on which that function's effectiveness depended, raising considerable problems for the criticism of Keats, both hostile and sympathetic. Hostile critics, in this sense, are neither heterodox nor antithetical but share the aesthetic under critique. Their complicity means that they cannot say what Keats is doing without joining in blowing the whistle on the common aesthetic's political function. Their criticism serves this political interest by becoming theoretically muted; my point is that such reticence still has *its* ideological point, and is thus indirectly expressed by the language of social animus which rushes in to fill the theoretical vacuum. The invective covers what Hazlitt, in a passage Keats quoted from his great attack on William Gifford, editor of the *Quarterly*, called 'the invisible link, that connects literature with the Police' (II, 72). However, paralleling this, sympathetic criticism can only point up Keats's political content by expounding the comprehensiveness of his aesthetic, and so also forgoing differentiation of that content.

The political is rather revealed by the way in which Keats's apparent lapses from poetry into supposedly lower, extra-literary registers are contained by the aesthetic, in accordance with its idealizing function. The fact that these lapses are not recuperable, or that the idealizing function becomes visible, means that the poetry's political, 'objective' critique immanently invokes a disabling self-critique. There is no Hegelian movement into a more historically apt coherence which can escape the inclusiveness of 'Romantic' art because it is prepared to abandon art altogether.[4]

What is objective about criticism here is that it is problematic. It cannot find an independent *point d'appui*, and what it unveils is a series of non-identities between aesthetics and politics: not an object but that object's dissolution through its immanent critique of its own consistency. The historical content in what follows consists of the failure of criticism, like the Kantian/Keatsian aesthetic, to secure its object. Therefore we must be vigilant to restore to these deconstructive victories their historical specificity. We are confronted with two heuristic modes which are equally aporetic *and* recuperative. The undermining of history through the deconstruction of its specificities is retrieved as a precisely historical experience of uncertainty – the historicity of history. The determination of the shape of deconstructive practice by historical circumstance is yet another productive defeat on which deconstruction thrives – the deconstruction of deconstruction. Because we cannot decide between these oppositions, both can claim the victory. The practical pay-off of this intellectual dilemma is that the reader can utilize whatever information emerges without having to adjudicate. To be outside one approach is to be inside both. As is repeatedly shown in the history of philosophy, surrender to its 'other' is only possible on philosophy's own terms. Absolutist pretensions, along with mutually pejorative characterizations, can be resisted in the name of both approaches. The real casualty ought to be neither deconstruction nor history but the opposition between the aporetic and the recuperative.[5] We will see that Keats's writing dissolves a comparable opposition, revealing how the aesthetic betrays (semiotically and polemically) the political and vice versa, each bringing the other to our notice as its dishonourable disguise.

Jerome McGann has pointed out criticism's neglect of the pun on 'leaf' in the first stanza of the 'Ode on a Grecian Urn'.[6] His reading compels us to see in the Ode a symptomatic paronomasia, the lateral movement of which creates an aesthetic within the aesthetic. This can be fairly obvious, as when the 'brede of marble men' implies that in the relief the urn pictures yet another art-work, either statuary or raised figures from another relief. 'Overwrought', the brede's key adjective, thus has at least four meanings. It describes the elevation of the 'brede' above the surface of the urn, the emotions of the 'mad pursuit' of 'men and maidens', the transference of figures from one work of art 'over' to another, and the overarching umbrage, itself legendary, fringing the urn's narrative. A word branching out in so many directions is itself overwrought, a fact that dramatizes yet again the poem's paronomastic tension. Or, the accuracy with which 'overwrought' describes itself disables that descriptive function. The word has been overworked beyond what is required, to excess, exhausted beyond usefulness.

This result is not, however, the rhetorical effect of an inevitable discrepancy between language's performative and descriptive functions. The reflexive pun thematizes the paradox attributed in Keats's poem to poetic authority. The justness with which the poem refers to itself, and specifically to its radically unauthorized signifying practice, is the means of its special pleading. What is typical of this art is its claims to typicality; all we need know about art is what it says about itself – and it says that too.

Such poetry exposes its limitations by doubling. It demonstrates its critical remove from what its aesthetic ideology obliges it to do by exhibiting the relativism inherent in its essentialist claims. This is a self-wounding critique, but possible none the less, and one which reflects upon the foundational model of all critique, Kant's critical philosophy. It does so by showing that the aesthetic remaining when critique has done its work is hermetic. It resists discursive parallels in so far as it lays claim to a universal humanism. To give, however, that humanism all the sensuous particularity which the Kantian aesthetic judgement permits is, as Schiller saw, to challenge the adequacy of other, discursive versions of human nature. At the same time, as Schiller did *not* see, this privileging of the immediate sensuous detail threatens the proclaimed self-sufficiency of the aesthetic. Keats, I think, lays bare a contradiction in the radical bias of Kantian aesthetics, a bias which Schiller develops. Keats's famed sensuousness is fuelled by an art which releases in us the desire that it *not* possess that imaginary function, the sphere of undetermined universality which allows it authority to educate our desires, but that it be, rather, a determinate judgement. Keats puts this point with a directness that courts the philosophical scandal involved: 'O for a Life of Sensations rather than of Thoughts!' (I, 185). Art educates us in wanting to realize the fulfilled humanity we can experience only aesthetically, without being inhibited by the need to observe the autonomy of art, which enabled us to intuit such emancipation in the first place.[7] Keats's poetry makes us want to possess the aesthetic experience it offers on terms which do not allow it to have generated such a desire. Once discovered in Keats's 'Monastry', 'Mammon' could never have belonged there. This impasse is at the heart of what I am calling Keatsian critique.

II

The opening of *Endymion*, John Wilson Croker's test-piece of Keatsian incompetence, is as tricky to read as the openings of Keats's later works. In its obsessive longing for the power to describe the effect of great art, the passage sets the tone for the narrative to come. In this, it continues the preoccupation of the preceding year's sonnets whose subjects include the experience of seeing the Elgin Marbles and not being up to describing the experience, and the frequent and apparently less problematic evocation of a feeling of inhabiting sensuously the literary space of a great tradition stretching from Chaucer, Dante and Petrarch, through Spenser and Milton to Chatterton, Wordsworth, Byron, Hunt and contemporary 'Great spirits'. As in the conclusion to 'The Eve of St. Agnes', temporal distance is used to promote an enabling pathos, whose touch confirms the reader's recognition of an erotic dilemma continuous with present energies. It elaborates the invitation to watch the vanishing point of the drowned Leander when, at the conclusion to the sonnet in his honour: 'He's gone! Up bubbles all his amorous breath.'

The obsession with matching inspirational influence to felt vocation, and the anxieties arising from possible disparities, tend to disguise the way in which Keats focuses another subject-matter. The advantage to Keats of taking other poems or artistic artefacts as his subject lies in the opportunity to close immediately, from the start, on the nature of aesthetic satisfaction. A deceptively simple point to be taken from these poems and from many of the earlier sonnets of 1816 is that to write of the experience of reading literature is to explore something continuous with other kinds of experience. In this Keats shows, as John Bayley claimed, that 'literature can become the most effective vehicle of reality'. In classic idealist fashion, to read is to attend to objects with such detachment that we become conscious of their naturalness (what Kant called purposiveness) or sheer appositeness to our experience of them with an intensity that somehow compensates for the otherwise tautological apprehension. 'It implies', in John Bayley's words, 'a kind of helpless being oneself.'[8] Keats, like Hegel, exposes the tautological character of idealist aesthetics, but without advancing from a phenomenological to an evaluative stance. In his early work there is a prophetic concentration on the effects of achieved works of art. The infinite regress of intertextual sources and authenticity (in the visual as well as the verbal arts) does not limit the meaning of Keats's recreation of the canonical line to a desire to belong to it. The corroborations, correlatives, catalogues, repetitions and velleities of Keats's sonnets allow him to feel through in a pre-critical manner what the aesthetic is meant to realize beyond the spectacle of its own construction. In all this there is a latent unease or restlessness with ideas of fulfilment and completion. Even in the most uncritical evocations of an environment of balmy hospitality centrally heated by literary musings, as in 'To one who has been long in city pent' or 'Oh, how I love, on a fair summer's eve', there is a tentative reach beyond pleasure into discontent. It is this that we sense in the final silence of 'an angel's tear', which, like the Satan alluded to in the title, 'falls through the clear ether', clouding the otherwise countrified content of the day-tripper in 'To one who has been long in city pent'. Or one might recall those figures of Puritan resistance, Milton and Sidney, whose 'stern forms' sit in silent judgement beside another 'delicious tear' with which 'Poesy' clouds the eye at the end of 'Oh, how I love, on a fair summer's eve'. Similarly, the catalogues that conclude other sonnets endeavour rather than succeed in suggesting the conclusiveness of their inventions. Lacking George Herbert's metaphysical 'something understood', they have to rely for credibility on their conspicuously imagined choice, an invitation to collude in the enjoyment of a world in which the anecdotal fronts as the essential. This risks tautology and redundancy, most startlingly in the daringly bathetic rounding off of the catalogue at the end of 'After dark vapours' with 'a poet's death'.

'The Beauties of . . .' is a predominantly eighteenth-century title which assumes the proportions of a gentlemanly knowledge of literature. Its rationale, however, gets progressively effaced in the Romantic period through the commonplace privileging of lyric over narrative, incident over plot, character over argument, and sympathetic imagination over discursive knowledge. One thinks, for example, of Keats's exemplary Kean, with his run of Shakespearian performances in a single season, each one transforming an entire play in the public imagination into *his* 'Othello', 'Hamlet', and so on. At the same time, though, the 'beauties' rhetoric of Keats's early verse, and especially *Endymion*, characterizes the text as a whole as a succession of achieved moments and quintessential distillations – the 'poetical concentrations' Leigh Hunt claimed Byron found unintelligible. 'Beauties ... in almost every page' were, after all, the mainstay of John Scott's rejoinder to the *Quarterly*'s review of *Endymion*.[9] As Keats tells Benjamin Bailey when well into the writing of *Endymion* in October 1817, 'I must make 4000 Lines of one bare circumstance and fill them with Poetry' (I, 169–70). 'Beauties' signals a kind of pure poetry – *Endymion*'s 'Poetry' – combatting in, for example, 'How many bards gild the lapses of time', the association of 'gilding' or beautifying with superficiality, and indicating instead Keats's un-Wordsworthian interest in the significance of result rather than process in art.

In a letter to Clough of 1852, Arnold senses this Keatsian effect of 'beauties' (which he also, ironically, attributes to Shelley) and shrewdly analyses its components. Arnold wants a modern poetry in which the diction serves the action. In Keats he finds a poet 'on a false track' because he sets himself

> to reproduce the exuberance of expressing the charm, the richness of images, and the felicity of the Elizabethan poets. Yet critics cannot get to learn this, because the Elizabethan poets are our greatest, and our canons of poetry are founded on their works. They still think the object of poetry is to produce exquisite bits and images.[10]

According to Arnold, by the middle of the nineteenth century Keats's success had come to inhibit criticism by forcing it to recognize the particularity of his poetry as the sensuous expression of a pure canonicity. Suddenly, he appears as the reactionary quintessence of orthodoxy, opposed by the radical Arnold with his innovatory hopes for a 'modern poetry'. Such a poetry, with its wider ambitions of becoming 'a complete magister vitae as the poetry of the ancients did', will move beyond the Romantic self-reflective habit towards an inclusive position of 'religious' authority, orientated towards 'the whole'. Ironically, in Arnold's story Keatsian 'beauties' have lost their pragmatic daring, just as the Elizabethans have been domesticated, and are getting in the way of critical progress. Keats's first critics were silenced theoretically by his style, but exactly because of the experiential consistency with which it made visible cultural prejudice and literary pre-understanding. However, norms which in his poetry become so visible, enjoying so palpable a design on us, may no longer be able to claim immunity from questioning or, in Hazlitt's terms, maintain the secrecy of their connection with Legitimacy. Keats may be unable to float the idea of a new canon, but he comes much nearer than Arnold does to showing how the canonical might be asked to prove its worth in another court. Terms like immediacy, intensity, proof on the pulses and touchstones all lose their tone of mute abandon when they can be seen to make up the vocabulary of fulfilment, and as their weaknesses can be seen to reflect upon the quality of the experience canonically rendered to us under the imprimatur of fulfilment.

What I hope is more evident now is the paradox by which Keats distanced or disqualified himself from canonical credentials through the very authority of his presentation of these credentials in the form of immediate aesthetic experience. Within one page or so of a letter to Haydon of May 1817, Keats, regarding his own work with some disgust, figures himself as 'one that gathers Samphire' while the 'Cliff of Poesy Towers above me' (alluding to a famous moment when Shakespearean language substitutes for the impossible scenery and is very much the thing itself) and then dares to conjure Shakespeare as his future presiding genius, thus typically showing himself to have participated in the elevation which puts him down (I, 242). When he equivocates comparably in the Preface to *Endymion* – 'the manner in which this poem has been produced ... will be quite clear to the reader, who must soon perceive great inexperience, immaturity, and every error denoting a feverish attempt, rather than a deed accomplished' – one of his hostile reviewers, Croker in the *Quarterly*, confesses that 'this does not appear to us to be *quite so clear* – we really do not know what he means.' John Gibson Lockhart, too, attacks the poem as defying rational commentary. But beneath the sustained gibe of unreadability, the hostile reviews' main trope,[11] lies a serious and understandable bafflement. When Keats's deprecation of his own work suggests it should be read as enjoining or 'denoting' a contrary intimacy with and loyalty to the protocols of high art, the politically hostile critic finds his target displaced. To deprecate the work is to take Keats's side, and so *another* reason must be found to account for critical resistance to Keats's presumptuous language of acquaintance.

It is this finesse which generates much of the heat in the early criticism of Keats, denying it the release of direct expression. The shortest way with *Blackwood's* and the *Quarterly* is to say that the overdetermined virulence grows out of this frustration, born in the Preface but nourished by the poem. Keats's supposed vulgarity was not a subversive *parody* of high art, precisely because it shared the same founding assumptions of the prevailing idealistic aesthetic. The deflection of criticism of the poem into criticism of the poet's Cockney presumption is what turns the poem into a parody; or, it is necessary to see the poem as a parody if the class attack on Keats is to legitimate itself as authentic criticism of his poem. It is this transformation that Levinson identifies and analyses. My concern here is with an order of Keatsian critique that required of the critics a foundational shift in order to keep unthinkable the idea that his critique might be non-parodic.

Although Lockhart's own writings of this period, *Peter's Letters to his Kinsfolk*, aspired to Swiftian satire of a sort, he had visited Germany (possibly in the company of the philosopher William Hamilton, later the Sir William Hamilton of Mill's *Examination*, much influenced by Kant) less than a year before his review of *Endymion*.[12] His trip was sponsored by William Blackwood for the purpose of translating F. Schlegel's *Vorlesungen über die Geschichte der alte und neue Literatur*, the last lecture (xvi) of which resumes the German idealist tradition and is full of admiration for Schiller and Fichte. Lockhart's idealist credentials are further supported by his admiration of Wordsworth and Coleridge. In *Peter's Letters*, Lockhart rejects *Blackwood's* caricature of Coleridge's 'German' obscurity in *Biographia Literaria*, and he praises that paradigm of Romantic irony, 'The Idiot Boy'.[13] The only way to resist the power of Keats's work to expose the contradictions of the idealist aesthetic (following Kant, the premise that we can only grasp fulfilment as tautology and that any superior ideal only has legislative authority provided it lacks executive authority) was to reveal the political function of those double binds. Of course the function's 'cover' lay in the problem of how to reveal a function that did not – could not – operate discursively, but only unconsciously and inarticulately beneath the unquestionable, end-stopped, transcendental valorizations rendered as Keatsian 'beauties'. This reticence followed from Kant's transcendental principle of judgement in accordance with which his aesthetic becomes the feeling for how extra-discursive reality is necessarily judged to be contingently organizing itself in discursive support. The implication here that one can therefore dovetail the sublime with the beautiful was seized upon as a prime tactic in counter-Revolutionary aesthetic ideology.[14] However, the resulting, asymptotic congruence between imaginative symbol and conceptual schema sets up the repetitive structure which leaves nothing more to be said. In accordance with the pattern I outlined at the start, to be outside discourse here again is to be doubly inside it. What Lockhart called the 'calm, settled, imperturbable' aspect of *Endymion*'s 'drivelling idiocy' froze reviewers in that pose of stymied aggression which they had to transform from theoretical bankruptcy into a new critical paradigm. *Endymion* so consistently enforced the immobility of their traditionally authoritarian stance that they now seem as defenceless to us as Keats must have appeared to them. Their ideological configuration is maintained by a self-censorship which paradoxically inhibits their critical defence. What was required was that their articulate attack on Keats's origins provide grounds for them not to take seriously his qualifications for having produced an immanent critique.

The vituperation Keats suffered had its own logic or pathology, vividly brought to light in Levinson's work. In every diminutive (Jack, Johnny, mankin, etc.) and sexual slur the reviewers betrayed their insensitivity to an involuntary satire on bourgeois self-sufficiency. Levinson's analysis of that displacement, and of its reconstitution as a legitimate critical focus on the poetry, is an account of what comes of a moment which the success of her reading uncovers as having been one of *Zugzwang*, in which any move is the wrong one. In foundational, Kantian terms, Keatsian sensuousness expresses the self-contradictory ideal to live a life constituted by his culture's regulative ideas. This match between felt, Keatsian 'excess' and prescriptive, Kantian 'impossibility' is the internally disruptive core to Keats's championing of high art. His aspiration to a here-and-now of artistic parity with the canonized poet in fact only exposes his culture's necessarily self-defeating notion of its own goals. To cast this aspiration as vulgar or *arriviste* is a way of isolating it from an endangered idealism. In practice, however, it produces a criticism open to a materialist, sociological analysis which leaves idealism behind. Yet it is the idealist aesthetic which makes sense of Keats's otherwise fatuous 'hungering', as Carlyle saw it, 'after sweets which he can't get'. It is the equation with Kantian aesthetics which most economically explains the words of the *British Critic*'s reviewer of *Endymion*, when he describes how Keats 'strikes from unmeaning absurdity into the gross slang of voluptuousness'.[15] In the history of attacks on Keats, this repeated juxtaposition of the charges of unintelligibility and sensuous vulgarity now leaves the impression of a tacit pact never to inquire if either fault might not take its complexion from the other.

III

Croker's difficulties with the opening of *Endymion* arose from his resistance to the poem's invitation that we join in a fiction whereby the flagrantly anecdotal is projected as the essential, and the full import of an idealist poetry is exposed. 'This', runs the fiction, 'is what fulfilment is like' – a symbolic adequacy of thought to object, the unproblematic assumption of necessity as one's own freedom, the experience of the random or miscellaneous as a significant catalogue, the whole rhetoric of comfort which directs the opening scenes of *Endymion*. Croker, I would suggest, disguises the poverty of this ideal by in effect claiming it has not happened: that it is not there to be observed and so cannot be judged. Keats's poem has, for him, the appearance of having been produced by 'an immeasurable game of *bouts-rimés*': this is to say, its equivalences are arbitrary and pat, the random result of auditory associations, risible as a Cockney parody of the heroic couplet and meaningless on the poem's own account.[16] The undoubted difficulties, however, in following the opening of *Endymion* arise from the effort of understanding a further possibility encompassing the qualities which Croker rightly senses, but allotting to them a place within another argument which he would have thought could not be formulated coherently. Since the theme of fulfilment is usually thought to exclude critique (critique being properly limited to the policing of the desire whereby fulfilment is to be achieved), the ultimate discontent suggested by a Keatsian critique of fulfilment can only appear to Croker as incompetence, ruled out of court by its successes. But, as I shall emphasize later, the critique of value is a common feature of contemporary economic discourse. Its bind is inescapable if you want to say something like the following: within Romantic aesthetics fulfilment, which only works as an idea in the normative, prescriptive realm, none the less has as its rationale the dissolution of that distinctiveness. Fulfilment is when an 'ought' becomes an 'is', but actually to present it as an 'is' may render it so ordinary as to make its previous, legislatory function quite incredible – hence the dissatisfied 'Was it for this . . .' which Wordsworth uses all his resources of poetic revision to restore. To preserve that legislative function, the power of aesthetic jurisdiction, it is best to keep fulfilment as the invisible endpoint of desire. It is this contradiction within the realist logic of fulfilment (in Kant's dialetic, 'the realism of the aesthetic finality of nature') which is exposed in Croker's and Lockhart's twin accusations of *Endymion*'s unintelligibility and vulgar sensuousness.

The poem's provocative dedication to Chatterton is a guide to the way Keats might have been thinking his way through his own abrasiveness. The dedication invites the reader to remember how Chatterton's youthful fraud is to create a language not natural to him, 'the stretchèd metre of an antique song'. This strange and insincere tongue is assimilated to the Romantic aesthetic when Chatterton is welcomed, as in Coleridge's 'Monody', as 'the young-eyed Poesy / All deftly mask'd as hoar Antiquity'. In Chatterton's case, the predominant taste *has* found it possible to escape the bind that if he is original, he is not antique; and if he is the genuine thing, he is not original. The parallel escape for Keats, given *Endymion*'s first reviews, would be from the certainty that if he is using a vocabulary of satisfaction, he cannot be critical of it; and if the effect *is* critical, he cannot be in command of his vocabulary.

The double-think required to escape the Keatsian bind is present at the start of *Endymion*, in its difficult opening transition:

> A thing of beauty is a joy for ever,
> Its loveliness increases; it will never
> Pass into nothingness, but still will keep
> A bower quiet for us, and a sleep
> Full of sweet dreams, and health, and quiet breathing.
> Therefore, on every morrow, are we wreathing
> A flowery band to bind us to the earth,
> Spite of despondence, of the inhuman dearth
> Of noble natures, of the gloomy days,

> Of all the unhealthy and o'erdarken'd ways
> Made for our searching – yes, in spite of all,
> Some shape of beauty moves away the pall
> From our dark spirits.
>
> (I, 1–13)

The pivotal 'Therefore on every morrow, are we wreathing' is puzzlingly reflexive. Who is doing the wreathing? Who is the narrator incorporating in the royal 'we' wreathing the 'thing of beauty'? The poem already appears tied to the task of simulating an image of aesthetic success – a poem about the experience of having read an aesthetically finished poem (good Wordsworthian precedents here). This is the Keatsian logic of catching up on an already poeticized landscape, a wilderness already 'dressed' by thought to facilitate the arrival of consciousness.

> And now at once, adventuresome, I send
> My herald thought into a wilderness –
> There let its trumpet blow, and quickly dress
> My uncertain path with green, that I may speed
> Easily onward, thorough flowers and weed.
>
> (I, 58–63)

The effect is to continue the earlier sonnets' view of the creation of poetic language as a place of repose: not a characterization of anything but, as in the 'Ode to Psyche', the dwelling on apprehension, the treatment of it as a place of arrival, John Jones's 'end-stopped feel'.[17]

In Kant's aesthetics, this kind of *aisthesis* permits the idea of the world as something that fortuitously coincides with the functioning of our faculties, an experience that dialectically bridges the gap between phenomena and things-in-themselves – 'a flowery band to bind us to the earth'. *Aisthesis*, or a complete relaxing of the cognitive functions for their sensuous contemplation, pleonastically invokes for Kant, as already suggested, the only legitimate notion of an external world that binds itself together as if to make possible our systematic understanding of it. The rhetorical equivalent of such a guarantee might be parataxis: the random catalogue of interchangeable descriptions indifferently standardized. What the paratactic version adds to the idea of getting on equivalent terms with essences is the suggestion that so absolute a guarantee of meaning actually deprives experience of a meaningful (syntactic) order. Nature now falls unnoticeably into place beneath its signs, and the alternative would be equally impossible to demonstrate. Along with this arises the need to repress the suggestion that anyone fobbed off on essentialist terms is being sold short. Cosmology in *Endymion* is inseparable from cosmetics, the 'known Unknown' carnally remystified by the poem's romance as 'Such darling essence' (II, 739–40). The opening passage of *Endymion* continues with a substantial, paratactic passage concluding in the unequivocal ascription of essence to its individual clauses, including the sequence which drove Croker to think of *bouts-rimés*:

>   Such the sun, the moon,
> Trees, old and young, sprouting a shady boon
> For simple sheep; and such are daffodils
> With the green world they live in; and clear rills
> That for themselves a cooling covert make
> 'Gainst the hot season; the mid-forest brake,
> And such too is the grandeur of the dooms
> We have imagined for the mighty dead,
> All lovely tales that we have heard or read –
> An endless fountain of immortal drink,
> Pouring unto us from the heaven's brink.
>
> Nor do we merely feel these essences
> For one short hour . . .
>   (I, 13–26)

Pan soon becomes the poem's principle of such a catalogue, a physical 'leaven' which dodges all conception and so escapes being part of mental 'dress', remaining the object of 'address' in the shepherds' hymn to him:

>   'Be still the unimaginable lodge
>   For solitary thinkings – such as dodge
>   Conception to the very bourne of heaven,
>   Then leave the naked brain; be still the leaven,
>   That spreading in this dull and clodded earth
>   Gives it a touch ethereal, a new birth;
>   Be still a symbol of immensity,

> A firmament reflected in a sea,
> An element filling the space between,
> An unknown – but no more!
> (I, 293–302)

Pan is the 'element filling the space between, the idea of a yeasty consistency behind differences, taken up in the indiscriminate stream of apostrophes to which the bright, essential Cynthia provokes Endymion in Book III (III, 52–102, 163–75), which raises also the idea of a benevolent nature. The paganism which reportedly offended Wordsworth's religious sensibilities seems too a convention under which a realism of fulfilment can be contemplated, and its unstable condition examined. Endymion, imagining 'happiness' as 'A fellowship with essence', is to be 'Full alchemized, and free of space' (I, 780), a solution that could be entirely ethereal, or, which might involve his transformation into a material form of infinite extension. The meaning will not settle and remains as oxymoronic as Endymion's dream of an archetypal union with Cynthia – 'O unconfined / Restraint! imprisoned liberty!' (I, 455–6). To have succeeded in writing a language which raises such equivocations about 'that completed form of all completeness . . . that high perfection of all sweetness' (I, 606–7) is by implication to have questioned the idea of fulfilment as the adequation of desire and, conversely, of desire as the striving for fulfilment. This conclusion either suggests an ideological component which can use the aesthetic idea of fulfilment for its own legislative ends, manipulating people's desires under false pretences which nevertheless seem inherent in the very logic of desire, and thus safe from criticism, their falsity expressible only as a kind of nonsense. Or else it suggests a willingness to accept the conventionally aberrant and unnatural as imaginative possibilities: following Adorno, we can experience in art the non-identity of things with their labels, an experience which promises the 'emancipation' of the aesthetic subject.[18] *Endymion*'s hostile critics drew both implications in their charges of nonsensical voluptuousness. Keats's own revision of the 'fellowship with essence' passage inspires his most explicit image of a critique of pleasure working through human variables.

My having written that Passage Argument will perhaps be of the greatest Service to me of any thing I ever did – It set before me at once the gradations of Happiness even as a kind of Pleasure Thermometer – and is my first Step towards the chief Attempt in the Drama – the playing of different Natures with Joy and Sorrow. (I, 218)

IV

So far, the possibilities for Keatsian critique have been largely passive, given shape through the accusations of the first hostile critics of his poems. But the reciprocal, revealing provocation which his writings offer to idealism should now be more visible. *Endymion* is a poem in which Keatsian intensity crowns the narrative far too soon. Endymion finds that he has 'raught / The goal of consciousness' early in the second of four books, and the precocious sexual continuation rather than realization of this achievement takes place before the end of book two. Yet the poem forestalls any straightforward discontent with its apparent structural mismanagement by foregrounding this intensity and overriding other disappointments through its claim to hold in focus a fugitive climax, and so to nudge us beyond the pleasure principle and into a critique of pleasure. The effect is to say: this is the goal of narrative, usually unquestioned, here brought forward for examination. The poem's psychological defence against critical discontent is a phenomenology of the tristitia consequent on pleasure.

Endymion's language of cultural acquaintance, in contrast to the deferential modesty of the published Preface, is strikingly ambitious in the possessiveness of its portrayal of 'the beautiful mythology of Greece'. This presumption takes the form of an intimate inwardness, physical and psychological, by which the empirical reach of Keats's poetic language exceeds its pictorial licence, at the same time foregrounding its poeticity. One thinks of Christopher Ricks's discussion of the 'slumbering pout' of *Endymion*'s Adonis or the 'limping hare' at the start of 'The Eve of St. Agnes'. Alternatively, Keats's self-signifying cultivation translates into endless circumscription which never closes on a classical centre because such closure is in general epistemologically impossible. Possession is inherently vicarious – Phoebe in place of Cynthia – and poetry is the aesthetic recognition or polemical redemption ('beauty is truth') of that otherwise unhappy fact. Both these versions of Keatsian sensuousness have had their skilful expositors.[19] What they return us to is the notion of a putative endpoint at which we are encouraged to apply what we take to be natural standards of experience to something we cannot have on those terms at all. This is a political as well as an epistemological point, and we have already discussed the politically advantageous self-deception which might be involved. But to expose such a tactic is to impugn the aesthetic collaborator, and in doing so Keatsian critique begins to go on the offensive. On the one hand, *Endymion*'s exaggerations suggest that such satisfaction is an impossible ambition of all art, and one which is, as a rule, decently repressed. On the other, Keats's importunate hyperboles conspicuously disguise the fact that if this view of art had its way, poetry would aspire to the condition of kitsch: an art which meets with no external resistance because it has been purified of all critical difference. This is the moral consequence of the Hegelian reading of the rhetoric of Kantian *aisthesis* quoted at the head of this chapter, a reading to which, Adorno concedes, Kant's formalism makes him vulnerable. The replicatory motives of *aisthesis* are so innocent – so disinterested – that they appear completely complacent in any but the most brazenly self-serving world. For readers who consider themselves cultivated, to meet with the implication that this is what they desire from their reading is highly insulting. It is as if Keats imagines a sudden access of expertise in which the esoteric reflexivity of avant-garde art becomes indistinguishable from the effortless self-evidence of kitsch: caviare for the general at last.[20]

Idealist bourgeois culture legitimates itself by constructing Keats as the *arriviste*, the importunate consumer of what is not for sale. He cannot buy into this culture because it is presented as the system which makes buying possible. This system is analogous to the ubiquitous symbolic order of exchange or credit which, from Simmel through Saussure to Foucault, rationalizes the *paroles* of individual monetary transactions; or, to the psychological blueprint which the Kantian tradition deduced and aesthetically savoured as the logical prerequisite of every act of determinate judgement or specific cognition. On either of these descriptions, political interest is disguised as the conditions under which a metaphysic is possible. The specifics of high bourgeois taste pose as an absolute regime – a universal – and it is the unchallengeable quality of this acculturation which converges embarrassingly with the self-exonerating logic of kitsch. One cannot change someone's taste for kitsch by pointing out the easiness or cheapness of the experience on offer, because it is just this facility of possession which is prized as the distinctive quality of the art.[21] To value kitsch knowingly, on the other hand, can be to express scepticism about any alternatives and, also, contempt for the naïve belief that more than an 'aura' survives of a sincerely humanist art claiming to escape comparison with kitsch. This is a modernist disingenuousness, reworked in postmodernism of all kinds from Warhol to Lyotard, which is not at all Keats's position. The modernist reader of Keats, however, is bound to see the connection and to find it useful in demonstrating the ways in which his writing escapes the straightforward recuperations of Romantic irony without simply amounting to the ineptitude and gaucheness attributed to it by his contemporary critics.

Writing of his suppressed Preface to *Endymion*, Keats describes his 'Public' as 'a thing I cannot help looking on as an Enemy', and claims that 'if there is any fault in the preface it is not affectation: but an undersong of disrespect to the Public.' In this context, the more a poet risks, not personally but on his own professional behalf, the further he pushes his readers into a position reflecting the endemic discomfiture of an audience positioned by an idealist aesthetic. It is hard, after all, to see how the Prefaces, published and unpublished, could be more modest on their author's part – the true function of a preface according to Keats's original version. Rather than a laboured and straightforward irony, Keats's persistent wish 'to conciliate men who are competent to look, and who do look with a zealous eye, to the honour of English literature' suggests that in so far as these critics represent public taste, to allow them to have their way – genuinely to conciliate them – is insult enough.

The provocation Keats offers to an idealist Romantic aesthetic makes it reveal its ideological basis in the analogy it bears to capital as a whole. As is the case with Schiller, the universals which are the stuff of aesthetic legitimacy are symbolic, like Kantian symbols, not just of morality but also inadvertently of the unquestionable efficacy of the credit on which bourgeois culture subsists. Keats's writing throws in relief the self-defeating character inflicted on art by this uncritical role. He does not produce independent critique but uncovers the equivalent of an uncritical moment in the critical philosophy, a disabling contradiction in the mastery with which art promotes its authoritative humanism. In this way he turns aesthetic success into its opposite, and symbolically calls into question the universals of which art is the acceptable expression and legitimating front. The possession of capital is, by analogy, made to seem accidental and disputable rather than the essential, unarguable right of the landed and mercantile classes.

This analogical reading adds to the picture of dominant members of a culture anxiously confronting in Keats's work the diminished importance their culture attributes to art. Art serves not as something which presents the content of fulfilment, but provides the excuse to go on believing in the possibility of utter satisfaction precisely because of the fact that it is never there. To propose, as Keats seems to do, a phenomenology of the ends of art is to reveal precisely that lack by visibly exploiting art as the discourse in which the relation of this discovery leaves us untroubled and reconciled. Art is given credit for what it cannot redeem; and to question this credit – to cause a 'run' on art – would be analogous to undermining confidence in the basic fiction by which those in possession of capital possess it by virtue of a universal interest in which all share. The force of Keats's conciliatory critique becomes even more palpable if we consider the contemporary crises of confidence in capital itself, crises whose character offers reinforcement to the aesthetic analogy from the other direction.

This happens especially where controversies over paper money are concerned. In economic debates of the time, value-making was not a Nietzchean overcoming of humanity, but a routine choice between contested options.[22] There is a long tradition in English philosophy and literature of distrust for and ridicule of the gradual ascendency of paper money over coin, dating from the establishment of the Bank of England in 1694 onwards. John Locke had been sure that money was 'a Pledge, which Writing cannot supply the place of . . . because a Law cannot give to Bills that intrinsic Value, which the universal Consent of Mankind has annexed to Silver and Gold'.[23] The notorious banking adventures of John Law on behalf of the Regent of France between 1716 and 1720 appeared to prove Locke right, and gave paper money a bad name and a satirical following, from Daniel Defoe's pamphlet on *The Chimera: or, The French Way of Paying National Debts* . . . (1720) to Thomas Love Peacock's *Paper Money Lyrics*. This last also associated paper money with imaginative activity, moving easily from laughter at the economic theorists of promissory notes to parodies of Southey, Wordsworth, Moore, Coleridge, Scott and Campbell. Peacock's collection develops the better-known literary scepticism of *The Four Ages of Poetry*. There, the poetic decline is measured in metals – iron, gold, silver and brass; it would seem reasonable to see no end to Peacock's loss of faith, and to construe *Paper Money Lyrics* as imaging the next stage in poetic debasement, 'the promiscuous rubbish of the present time to the exclusion of the select treasures of the past'.[24] As Peacock's double-edged satire confirms, Law's monetary practices (issuing money to stimulate trade, but causing vast inflation and an unstoppable run on his bank) may have been discredited, but his 'superior genius', as Sir James Steuart was to call it, and basic tenets of his theory were not.[25] The inherent organicism of such theories, according to which the national circulation of money was analogous to the corporeal circulation of the blood, was attractive to would-be philanthropists, motivated primarily by considerations of social rather than fiscal health, as much as to selfish speculators. Both approved of Law's wish that 'by this money the people might be employed'.[26] George Berkeley, in his *Querist* (1735–7), scandalized by the thought that he might belong to 'the only people ['our Irish'] who may be said to starve in the midst of plenty' can find no 'vertue in gold or silver, other than as they really set people at work, or create industry'.[27] Hume investigated further the benefits of monetary circulation, but his belief that money, 'having chiefly a fictitious value, the greater or less plenty of it is of no consequence', is offset by his suspicions 'concerning the benefits of *banks* and *paper-credit*'.[28] He might have felt justified in his fears by what happened to the English economy from 1797 to 1819. As Levinson has observed, these years embrace almost the exact duration of Keats's lifetime when, faced with the additional demands of financing the Napoleonic Wars, the government passed a Restriction Act prohibiting the Bank of England from redeeming any of its notes in gold, legislation which held from 1797 until 1819. Even in 1819, only the palliative measure of David Ricardo's Ingot Plan was adopted, and none but relatively large amounts of cash could be redeemed, and then only in bullion, not in coin. Of the 2,028 bars made for this purpose, nicknamed 'Ricardoes', only thirteen were sold, mainly because the market price fell below the mint price and buyers in the short term lost money. Full convertibility resumed only in 1823. By a striking corroboration, therefore, in Keats's productive years 'the realms of gold' would provide the perfect image of the imaginary wealth of literary inheritance, while showing that it would be wiser to stay in credit there, on paper, than to seek a more tangible and realistic standard of value.[29]

Most economic historicans seem agreed that it is, after all, very doubtful if the English economy could have borne the financial burdens imposed by the Napoleonic Wars had it not adopted the device of the Restriction Act and declared Bank of England notes to be legal tender irrespective of the availability of securities. The *Edinburgh Review* opposed Ricardo and the 'bullionists' who wanted to limit the domestic money supply and thus facilitate a return to the gold standard. Ricardo took Adam Smith's disapproval of devaluation as precedent, and could have cited Frances Hutcheson in support.[30] In *Queen Mab*, the young Shelley shows himself an out and out bullionist. In *The Mask of Anarchy* he continues to attack paper credit as another form of disenfranchisement, straightforwardly opposing its exchange-value to workers' labour-value.

> Paper coin – that forgery
> Of the title deeds which ye
> Hold to something of the worth
> Of the inheritance of the earth
> (xlv)

Keats, on the other hand, is a poetic inflationist; one whose work suggests that 'the inheritance of the earth' will become more available through the spread of a credit by which, in the inflationary terms of Law, Berkeley and occasionally Hume, 'the people may be employed'.[31] Logically, however, Ricardo made it as embarrassing as possible for the anti-bullionists to defend the expansion of paper credit. In his Appendix to *The High Price of Bullion*, he asks his opponent from the *Edinburgh Review*: 'is it conceivable that money should be sent abroad for the purpose merely of rendering it dear in this country and cheap in another, and by such means to ensure its return to us?'[32] Clearly it was, and, transposed to the economics of the aesthetic, such pragmatism could be equally sophistical and compromising. Arguably, Keats, in the eyes of *Endymion*'s hostile reviewers, had demonstrated the perversity of Ricardo's logic to the letter. First, he showed that the aesthetic experience of ultimate good depended for its unique value on having been 'sent abroad', deferred to some ideal, irredeemably exemplary realm. Secondly, through his 'promiscuous' exploration of these aesthetic ends (that is, the hedonistic phenomenology of satisfaction and fulfilment), Keats cheapened them sufficiently to remind readers of their justifiable expectation of enjoying them back in the here and now. Keats's 'speculative Mind', as a passage in his letter to the George Keatses of February–May 1819 shows, carries a Wordsworthian universal, 'one human heart', to its shockingly democratic conclusion without fear of debasement – 'the pity is that we must wonder at it; as we should at finding a pearl in rubbish' (II, 80). Not to accept the reality of 'speculations', and to lack the courage 'to put down his halfseeing', is how Keats's poet 'makes a false coinage . . . poetry that has a palpable design upon us – and if we do not agree, seems to put its hand in its breeches pocket'. Bad poetry, that is, abandons credit to buy readers off in kind (I, 223–4).[33]

In the context of Keats's aesthetic economy, 'credit' is less the institutional embodiment of desire through 'the perpetual deferral of one's returns' (as David Simpson accurately ascribes it to Wordsworth) than the challenge offered to 'value' by a suddenly empowered consumerism. In this critical complicity, Keats contrasts more sharply yet with Blake's frequent and visionary use of monetary imagery, seen by Kurt Heinzelman to engineer 'a momentary triumph over economic discourse'.[34] Ricardo's satirical picture, exposing the duplicitous versatility of capital which enabled the economy to survive its greatest crisis, was innocently reflected back to the reviewers less than a decade later by Keats's poetry. Significantly, Croker was later stung to write a pamphlet resuming the history of financial crises from Law onwards, and claiming the superiority of the Scottish banks over the English banks in maintaining the value of small paper credit.[35] Croker's anxiety sheds further light on the fury aroused by Keats's skewed conformity and harmlessly conciliatory ambitions. The mapping of financial upon aesthetic interests when Ricardo's diagnostic picture is superimposed upon Keats's is unsurprising. As Karl Niebyl has argued, 'a theory of money must... be an aspect of general economic theory, the latter being itself, or being an aspect of, a dynamic theory of social organisation'. And Levinson proves that in the 'economic allegory' of the 'Hyperion' poems and 'Lamia' the 'structural contradictoriness of money' reflects 'the contradictions in Keats's experience'.[36] Theories of money are not static hypotheses but historical explanations whose relativity is only visible in their dependency on other cultural factors. Recent criticism which has usefully explored the common fiduciary and figural logic of financial and aesthetic economies has perhaps insufficiently stressed that it is our inheritance of aspects of a specific, Romantic aesthetic and its capitalist affiliations which makes it true that, in Marc Shell's words, 'for us the terrible dictum – that nothing will come of nothing – seems to hold true. Except, that is, in the shadowy realms of aesthetics and monetary policy.'[37] To understand how Keats's 'realms of gold' might in effect dispel these shadows is to understand the scandalous fit between his poetry and the contemporary economics of financial survival.

V

Keats's immanent critique of the Romantic aesthetic is powered by his writing's exposure of the fact that its hedonistic credit is irredeemable, and that attempts to redeem aesthetic promise are treated as misunderstandings of the best way to put its fictional wealth to work. The Keatsian example shows that this defence cuts both ways, since the use of art to preserve the idea of transcendental imperatives with categorical claims on our essential nature is now married to a disreputable, inflationary disregard for an economy which thus balances the normative and the natural in opposite columns. Keats's sensuousness and vulgarity dispense with the niceties of idealist bookkeeping and propose phenomenological satisfactions in the speculative field. This is the unacceptable face of an aesthetic which in theory sanctions this proposal, but always under the semblance of economic responsibility. In (Kantian) theory, adventures in the intelligible world can only be recalled in terms which judge without determining a universality bathetically fitting the world of natural appearances; and natural desire is similarly policed by this hypothetical convergence with its regulative ideals. However, to cash the bond by innocently imagining a fulfilment realized threatens the economy's credit by placing under scrutiny the value of its redemption. At best, a cosmetic gloss is spread over its tautologies and parataxes, making them more acceptable but still showing how plenitude can shade into kitsch. To ignore the economy's assumed security of *specie* is, then, to beat it at its own game, enjoying on credit what could never possibly be paid for in kind – kind, that is, as defined according to prescriptions of the natural before the ideal spending-spree began.

Art of this kind is not so much an allegory of reading, as criticism following the work of Paul de Man might see it. By that I mean an allegory reinscribing the disfigurations (exercises in catachresis) by which we supposedly produce the literal. Such art is better cast as an allegory of art. It reinscribes the ideology whereby we agree to accept the impossibility of the literal (the whole, the unconscious, or whatever we choose to call heterogeneity for the moment) provided this loss is told to us in art. We are thus content to get our only glimpse of another possibility in the condescension art shows to us for this purpose. One might see in this model an adaptation of Wordsworth's ingratiating foster mother, 'Nature', but shorn of all her metaphysics, and knowingly aestheticized – as though tales of that forgotten 'imperial palace whence [we] came' reflected on her mollifying power to market her compensations with such success as to make indistinguishable from them any wish for something more.

This 'reflection' comes nearest to having an independent, critical substance in the staging of the openings of the 'Hyperion' poems, when they are read as a resumé of Keats's immanent critique of the sublime redundancy of the Romantic aesthetic, the divine sameness by which it recuperates the aporetic, simultaneously inside and outside its own rhetorical project. 'Hyperion' conjures up the availability of a heroic tradition, the enormity of whose imminence has a petrifying effect. The shape of this pressure is initially given through the poem's temporality, or rather its atemporality, in anticipation of that paralysing *nunc stans* which freezes and monumentalizes the kinetic efforts of its actors and narrators in a series of achieved moments and sculpted poses. The isolation which the opening sentence of 'Hyperion' exposes grows more intimate and assured as, again almost in parody of Wordsworth's 'Ode', it slips into an inwardness 'Far' from the common coordinates of everyday experience – 'morn', 'noon', 'eve'. This interiorization does not consequently take on the temporal form of inner sense: there has been no Wordsworthian movement through memory to arrive at this place and so measure its depth. Rather, the vale pictures what it is to obviate all motion, all desire. The landscape apparently described is in fact telescoped into images of its own lack of identifying temporal or spatial perspective. To be 'quiet as a stone' is to be so unsurprisingly quiet as to be quiet *simpliciter*: a stone without a dynamic moment or an energizing context because it has absorbed all such as qualities of its own massive equilibrium. The rhetoric of this state is sheer tautology, as in the extended pleonasm with which Thea evokes the Titans' inner life as one of undifferentiated externalization: 'O moments big as years! / All as ye pass swell out the monstrous truth, / And press it so upon our weary griefs / That unbelief has not a space to breathe.' Truth so protracted can only reiterate its own mass or extension; there is no room for the temporal or spatial progression necessary to Wordsworthian revision. We now realize that what we are 'far' from, what we are distanced from, is again distance itself. 'Forest on forest hung above his head / Like cloud on cloud' not necessarily because of some fancied visual resemblance between a cumulus of cloud and a formation of trees or hyperbolic foliage vertically stacked, but, more likely, in a proleptic expression of the stillness, 'No stir of air', in which clouds could occupy so stationary a pose. In this quality of fixture it is as if existence has become a predicate, and predicates repeated take on another life. When the 'shade' of Saturn's 'fallen divinity' deadens the voiceless stream, it deadens it 'more', enhancing rather than extinguishing an intrinsic quality; the Naiad's finger was already at her lips for it to be pressed 'closer'. The undisturbable presence of things is used to impoverish the language which, the poem persuades us, has successfully presented them. The tautologous description that opened the second paragraph – 'Along the margin-sand large foot-marks went, / No further than to where his feet had strayed' – is, first, a provocatively unremarkable mapping of the perfect fit of sign and thing, mark and foot. But more than this is the implication of the nugatoriness of epistemological fulfilment and its aesthetic correlatives. Give this language the authority it desires, in which signification is entirely informative and appearance statuesque, and watch it settle into a rhetoric of redundancy. Similarly, an impossibly reflexive ode to the psyche, which already is ('the wreathed trellis of a working brain') the mind it purports to address, tries to euphemize its tautology by becoming an 'Ode to Psyche'.

 The rest of 'Hyperion' works on the possibility of something else, something strained for in the early move from pleonasm into the chiasmus describing Thea's expression: 'But O! how unlike marble was that face, / How beautiful, if sorrow had not made / Sorrow more beautiful than Beauty's self.' Rhetorically flexed in this way, the tautologies of 'Hyperion' try to curb their own self-sufficiency and restore a meaningful difference between themselves and their object, impossibly revealing themselves 'frail / To that large utterance of the early Gods'. Yet the outcome, tragically, falls once more into repetition, and in 'The Fall' the further internalization of action within Moneta's brain can only resume the same old Titanic story, the start of 'Hyperion'. However, the cul-de-sac is already sketched in the openings of both poems, in the show of a criticism trapped within the ironic elaboration of what it cannot distance, possessing a conscious but unforthcoming insincerity. This dilemma is developed by Saturn's apparent recourse to another perhaps only closer language, the 'mother tongue' taken up in the opening of 'The Fall'. With hindsight, the reader can take Saturn 'listening to the Earth, / His ancient mother, for some comfort yet' as listening for a story different from that of the 'high tragedy', in which the poet of 'The Fall' has to be initiated and which has brought him to this low and deep realization of its archetype. The 'Hyperion' poems can easily appear to blend into the common currency of Romantic irony; but, closely read, the poems expose irony's impoverished fulfilment and incorrigible reflexivity. They begin to negotiate the surrender of such self-identity for something less assured, something not inevitably recuperable through the ironies of poetic self-criticism. By the opening of 'The Fall', the 'mother tongue' has become the democratic franchise of 'every man whose soul is not a clod', in explicit contrast to elitist, a priori prescriptions of who can and cannot be a poet. Fanatic, savage and poet differ only in powers of articulation, and the resources of articulateness lie in the *mamaloschen*. The only content ascribed to the poet's 'dreams' and 'visions' comes from the utopian impulse of others, of fanatics who 'weave / A paradise for a sect' or the savage who 'Guesses at Heaven'. Poetry has no content of its own, hence its inability to legislate on its own account and its deference to posterity for its definition. Poetry is nothing but the name given to the effective expression of something better than there is by those who have been educated ('nurtured') in their native language. The narrator's concession at the end of the paragraph – 'Whether the dream now purposed to rehearse / Be Poet's or Fanatic's will be known / When this warm scribe my hand is in the grave' – is a paradox which appears covertly to reinforce the nothingness attributed to poetry by the logic of the argument so far. In other words, whatever happens, 'the dream now purposed to rehearse' is in language, and any subsequent soubriquet of 'poetry' can only appear honorific or supernumerary. Abandoning the whole 'Hyperion' project, Keats writes that it is 'English', not an 'artful' poetry, which 'ought to be kept up' (II, 167).

To read the opening of 'The Fall' in this way seems to go against the grain of Keats's poetic ambitions, ambitions caught in that final dedication to posterity, however vulnerable. But again it is worth emphasizing that even this bid for retrospective legislation masks or euphemizes a present lack. The effacement of distance, spatial and temporal, which produces the redundancies of the opening of 'Hyperion' is here reproduced within another, more Hegelian conundrum. If the poem will only be recognizable as poetry by a later age, it is not poetry now; yet a concession which can only be formulated in the future is one impossible to write in the poem's present, a concession impossible to have conceded. The narrator is trying to cover up his really disturbing surrender of poetic authority to the 'mother tongue' with an artificial crisis. Seeing through this artifice suggests that poetry and articulateness are the same thing after all; 'English' is the English of Chatterton (II, 167, 212); to question the poetry in one's writing produces a specific kind of poem rather than another form of writing. It is like writing an ode ('Ode on Indolence') in which poetry is one of the options that the poem's 'nothingness' circumscribes, as opposed to writing in an explicitly low or rebellious idiom. Keats's isolated attempt in that vein is 'the Spirit of Outlawry' of the Robin Hood lyrics, a sally quickly contained again within the literary nostalgia of 'Lines on the Mermaid Tavern'. The Mermaid Tavern's common table comfortably hosts Robin's pre-bourgeois idyll of emancipation ('Since men knew not rent nor leases') within an Elizabethan literariness – an imagined unobtrusiveness allowing poetry to startle 'not with itself but with its subject', while remaining uneffaced by its success (II, 224). There is enough in this and in the opening of 'The Fall' to show both that poetry is potentially at hazard, and that characteristic of this kind of poetry is perpetually to simulate such crises on its own terms, so that it may have a stake in their plausibility. Keats dramatizes in this way the impossibility of his own parabasis and the gains and losses of a historical appreciation which will be able to see the poetry, but only at the cost of being able to take the aesthetic crisis seriously.

We cannot take idealism at its own estimation of itself, and so we fail to be limited by and thus true to the constraints of Keats's aesthetic. We see the manner in which his critique and its self-censorship are bound together. We see too what Keats could not when his conspicuously euphemistic and cosmetic style negates his writing's ostensible ideological conformity. By then, however, his aesthetic credit is exhausted. We have to move on to another critical standard. In socially genetic terms, the 'Hyperion' poems situate Keats closest to a class whose radical moment has passed with the French Revolution, and whose effaced sign of a former radical interest is the commercial credit it enjoys as a result of the same economic shifts more peacefully achieved in England. As critique, Keats's poetry portrays the ersatz establishment thus created 'To the most hateful seeing of itself'. But, above all, what is peculiar about such inauthenticity is the inscribed suggestion that there is no alternative; and the tragic strength of the 'Hyperion' poems is their euphemistic betrayal of the historical fact that, within their aesthetic, criticism and creation, disownment and renewal, abandonment and progress have to take place in the same words, through the same effects, powered by the same talents, clenched in the same narratives.

Notes

References to Keats's poems are to *The Poems of John Keats*, edited by Miriam Allott (London and New York: Longman, Norton, 1970). Quotations from the letters come from *The Letters of John Keats: 1814–21*, edited by Hyder E. Rollins, 2 vols (Cambridge, Mass.: Harvard University Press, 1958).

1. Susan Wolfson, 'Introduction' to 'Keats and Politics: a Forum', *Studies in Romanticism*, vol. 25, no. 2 (Summer 1986), p. 171.
2. Marjorie Levinson, *Keats's Life of Allegory – the Origins of a Style* (Oxford: Basil Blackwell, 1988), pp. 291, 23, 5–6, 141.
3. I am here following Hannah Arendt's interpretation of Kant's third *Critique* as containing 'perhaps the greatest and most original aspect of Kant's political philosophy . . . Culture and politics, then, belong together because it is not knowledge or truth which is at stake, but rather judgement and decision, the judicious exchange of opinion about the sphere of public life and the common world', *Between Past and Future* (New York: Viking Press, 1961), pp. 219–24. Pierre Bourdieu, in *Distinction. A Social Critique of the Judgement of Taste*, trans. R. Nice (London, Melbourne and Henley: Routledge & Kegan Paul, 1984), sees a relation between Kant's separation of taste from the bodily and his separation of art from kitsch or 'schmaltz'. Bourdieu thinks the separation can only be maintained by a sublimation of the lower, 'popular' term by the 'higher', bourgeois one. The consequence when this sublimation, in working, wears thin is the subject of my chapter, rather than the straight confrontation with bourgeois aesthetics engineered by Bourdieu's sociology of taste. Bourdieu criticizes Derrida's critique, in *La vérité en peinture*, of Kant's third *Critique*: 'Because he never withdraws from the philosophical game, whose conventions he respects, even in the ritual transgressions at which only traditionalists could be shocked, he can only philosophically tell the truth about the philosophical text and its philosophical reading, which (apart from the silence of orthodoxy) is the best way of not telling it . . .' (p. 493). In Bourdieu's convergence of opposites here, Derrida could only preserve his oppositional stance by critically energizing 'the silence of orthodoxy', much as he does 'sous rature' in *De la grammatologie*. It is a similar response to Bourdieu that I have tried to elicit for Keats. Derrida, of course, would hardly regard his own work as exhausting a paradigm in preparation for cultural materialism. For a fuller and brilliant handling of these subjects, see Terry Eagleton's forthcoming work on aesthetics.
4. See *Hegel's Aesthetics: Lectures on Fine Art by G. W. F. Hegel*, trans. T. M. Knox, 2 vols (Oxford: Clarendon Press, 1975), vol. I, pp. 524–9; I think Richard Rand uncovers the same history when he links the ambitious improprieties of Keatsian 'translation' of all kinds – metamorphosis, conveyancing, displacement, dissemination – to an immanent attack on a 'neoclassical' aesthetic and on our own 'classical' modes of reading it. See 'o'er-brimm'd', *Oxford Literary Review*, vol. 5, nos 1 and 2, pp. 42–3, 53–5; and 'Ozone: an essay on Keats', *Post-Structuralist Readings of English Poetry*, ed. Christopher Norris and Richard Machin (Cambridge: Cambridge University Press, 1986), pp. 294–307.

5 Most of the contributions to the recently published extended debate on the subject, *Post-structuralism and the Question of History*, ed. Derek Attridge, Geoff Bennington and Robert Young (Cambridge: Cambridge University Press, 1987), seem to have this consequence. Geoff Bennington, however, while attacking the 'absent' transcendentalism of aporetic logic, concludes a sustained criticism of Terry Eagleton's 'liberal' or pragmatic ('Machiavellian' might be better) historicism with a blatant bid for superiority which sacrifices information for the purposes of maintaining opposition – see especially p. 27.
6 Jerome McGann, *The Beauty of Inflections* (Oxford: Clarendon Press, 1985), pp. 44–5.
7 Friedrich Schiller, *On the Aesthetic Education of Man* in a series of letters, edited and translated with an introduction by Elisabeth M. Wilkinson and L. A. Willoughby (Oxford: Clarendon Press, 1967). See Peter Bürger, *Theory of the Avant-garde*, trans. Michael Shaw with an introduction by Jochen Schulte-Sasse (Minneapolis: University of Minnesota Press, 1984), especially pp. 44–6.
8 John Bayley, 'Keats and Reality', *Proceedings of the British Academy* (1962), pp. 118, 98.
9 Kean's popularity and commercial success is emphasized in biographies of him as much as the distinction with which, in B. W. Proctor's near-contemporary *Life*, he impressed '*character* on almost everything which he attempted'. Proctor refers to both under the Keatsian rubric of 'Return of the Golden Age'. He also describes how Kean typically 'determined to make the hero the most conspicuous object in the play', and helps show how Kean's egoism, so apparently different from Keatsian 'disinterestedness', could none the less provide the example for Keats's literary utilitarianism. Bertram Joseph, in *The Tragic Actor* (London: Routledge & Kegan Paul, 1959), could be describing Keatsian practice when he catalogues Hazlitt's and contemporary critics' accounts of Kean's seizing on 'the parts' of a character, sometimes to the neglect of 'the broad and massy effect', but often in order to translate a character 'with great freedom and ingenuity into a language of his own'. Too great a sacrifice of the integrity of line and plot to climactic 'points' resulted in 'a clap-trap' or precocious fulfilment retrievable only in a performance of what Crabb Robinson called 'pure feeling' (pp. 265–6, 275). Byron's remark is in Leigh Hunt's *Lord Byron and Some of his Contemporaries* (London, 1828), p. 266. For Scott's defence, see *Keats: the Critical Heritage*, ed. G. M. Matthews (London: Routledge & Kegan Paul, 1971), p. 116. Other reviewers focus on *Endymion*'s 'beauties' and describe its 'poetical concentrations' as 'flowers of poetry' or 'pure poetry' (Francis Jeffrey, ibid., pp. 203–4); 'if it be not, technically speaking, a poem', concludes Patmore, it 'is poetry itself', ibid., p. 135. The burlesque of Hunt's and Keats's style by 'Beppo' in the *Literary Journal* (20 March 1819, p. 92) – 'Pleasant Walks; A Cockney Pastoral, In the manner of Leigh Hunt, Esq.' – transforms the second line of Hunt's sonnet 'To John Keats' ('Whose sense discerns the loveliness of things') into ''Tis well I see the beautiful of things', making this distillation its refrain, and extracting most of its humour from the miscellaneous quality of 'Cockney'

catalogues. See Lewis M. Schwartz, *Keats Reviewed by his Contemporaries: a Collection of Notices for the Years 1816-21* (Metuchen, NJ: Scarecrow Press, 1973), pp. 151–5.

10 *Critical Heritage*, p. 326.

11 *Critical Heritage*, p. 111; the reviewer (probably Richard Woodhouse) in *The Champion*, 8 June 1818, recognizes and describes the unmethodical habit: 'Let [the reviewers] . . . refer to principles: let them show us the philosophic construction of poetry, and point out its errors by instance and application . . . If, however, they follow their old course, and having tackled the introduction of the first book, to the fag end of the last, swear the whole is an unintelligible jumble . . .', *Critical Heritage*, pp. 87–8.

12 For the extent of German influences on Lockhart, see G. Macbeth, *John Gibson Lockhart – a Critical Study* (Urbana: University of Illinois Press, 1935), pp. 62–83. Francis R. Hart gives a helpful account of the Coleridgean tendency of Lockhart's writings in *Lockhart as Romantic Biographer* (Edinburgh: Edinburgh University Press, 1971): 'Peter . . . comes equipped with a Coleridgean "idea" of Scotland', p. 56. Lockhart could later write a crudely antisemitic review of Heine's *De l'allemagne* in the *Quarterly* on the basis of a warped understanding of nationalistic elements in Herder's and the Schlegels' writings ('Heine on Germany', December 1835, vol. 55, pp. 1–34); but his ambition in 1825 of 'throwing materials of History into the ever attractive form of Biography' (Hart, p. 25) shows the Carlylean part he played in the general diffusion of idealism in Britain. Sir William Hamilton's 'On the Philosophy of the Unconditioned', *Edinburgh Review*, vol. 50, no. 99 (1829), pp. 194–221, engages directly with Kant and Schelling. See also René Wellek, *Immanuel Kant in England* (Princeton, NJ: Princeton University Press, 1931). Wellek's magisterial dismissal of English attempts to understand Kant has perhaps led subsequent commentators to underestimate the extent to which German idealism worked itself into English Romantic sensibility, despite Wellek's equal emphasis on the variety of ways in which Kant was assimilated, however inaccurately. For Wellek, Sir William Hamilton 'genuinely assimilated some of Kant's thought and appropriated some of his ideas for his own purposes' (p. 51).

13 *Peter's Letters to his Kinsfolk*, 3 vols (Edinburgh, London and Glasgow, 1819), vol. II, pp. 144–5; vol. I, pp. 176–7.

14 See Ronald Paulson's discussion of its Burkean sources in *Literary Landscape: Turner and Constable* (New Haven, Conn. and London: Yale University Press, 1982), pp. 147–8; and Theresa M. Kelley's excellent analyses of its dominant Wordsworthian forms in *Wordsworth's Revisionary Aesthetics* (Cambridge: Cambridge University Press, 1988).

15 *Critical Heritage*, p. 94.

16 Ibid., p. 112; see William Keach's useful discussion of Keats's couplets, 'Cockney Couplets: Keats and the Politics of Style', in 'Keats and Politics: a Forum', *Studies in Romanticism*, vol. 25, no. 2 (Summer 1986), pp. 182–96.

17 John Jones, *John Keats's Dream of Truth* (London: Chatto & Windus, 1969).

18 Theodor Adorno, *Aesthetic Theory*, trans. C. Lenhardt, ed. Gretel Adorno and Ralph Tiedemann (London and New York: Routledge & Kegan Paul, 1984), p. 113.

19 C. Ricks, *Keats and Embarrassment* (Oxford: Clarendon Press, 1974), pp. 13ff; M. Aske, *Keats and Hellenism: an Essay* (Cambridge: Cambridge University Press, 1986).
20 See Clement Greenberg's discussion in 'Avant-garde and Kitsch' (1939) in *Art and Culture* (London: Thames & Hudson, 1973), p. 14; for Keats's use of 'caviare' see McGann, *The Beauty of Inflections*, pp. 32–9.
21 I am trying here to expand on Adorno's remarks in *Aesthetic Theory* – 'Implicit in the concept of art is the phenomenon of kitsch' (p. 175), 'It lies dormant in art itself' (p. 339), 'A critique of kitsch, if it is radical and unrelenting, passes beyond kitsch and encompasses art *per se*' (p. 435), and also pp. 53, 70–1; see also Stephen Bungay's brief but helpful discussion in *Beauty and Truth: a Study of Hegel's Aesthetics* (Oxford: Clarendon Press, 1984), p. 95.
22 See, for example, Ricardo's summary of the problem in the chapter on 'Value and Riches, their Distinctive Properties', in *The Principles of Political Economy and Taxation* (1817), introduced by Donald Winch (London: Dent; 1973) – 'Many of the errors in political economy have arisen from errors on this subject, from considering an increase of riches, and an increase of value, as meaning the same thing, and from unfounded notions as to what constituted a standard measure of value' (p. 183). Equally relevant to Keats would be Thorstein Veblen's critique of the 'pecuniary canons of taste' of the *nouveaux riches* for whom 'terms in familiar use to designate categories or elements of beauty are applied to cover this [otherwise] unnamed element of pecuniary merit': *The Theory of the Leisure Class – an Economic Study of Institutions* (1899), introduced by C. Wright Mills (London: Unwin Books, 1970), p. 108. Keatsian 'diligent indolence' similarly parallels the capitalism and aesthetics of a class for whom, in Veblen's description, 'leisure is the conventional means of pecuniary repute' (p. 49).
23 John Locke, 'Some Considerations of the Consequences of the Lowering of Interest and Raising the Value of Money . . .' (1691), in *Several Papers Relating to Money, Interest and Trade, &c.* (London, 1696), p. 32.
24 *The Halliford Edition of the Works of Thomas Love Peacock*, ed. H. F. B. Brett-Smith and C. E. Jones, 10 vols (London: Constable, 1924–34), vol. VII, pp. 95–147.
25 Sir James Steuart, *An Inquiry into the Principles of Political Oeconomy* (1767), ed. A. S. Skinner 2 vols (Edinburgh and London: Oliver & Boyd, 1966), vol. I, p. 479.
26 John Law, *Money and Trade Considered: with a Proposal for Supplying the Nation with Money* (Edinburgh, 1705), p. 11.
27 G. Berkeley, *Querist* (1735–7), part I, p. 32.
28 D. Hume, *Essays Moral, Political and Literary*, ed. T. H. Green and T. H. Grose, 2 vols (London: Longmans, Green, 1875), vol. I, pp. 321, 311; for Hume as a moderate inflationist, see his approval of increasing the money supply if it 'keeps alive a spirit of industry in the nation, and increases the stock of labour, in which consists all real power and riches' (vol. I, p. 315).
29 See Michael J. Gootzeit, *David Ricardo* (New York and London: Columbia University Press, 1975), pp. 2, 22.
30 Ricardo, *Economic Essays*, ed. E. C. K. Gonner (London: Frank Cass, 1923), p. 40; see also W. L. Taylor, *Francis Hutcheson and David Hume as Predecessors of*

Adam Smith (Duke, NC: Duke University Press, 1965).
31 See Douglas Vickers, *Studies in the Theory of Money 1690–1776* (London: Peter Owen, 1960), p. 133; Gareth Stedman Jones, *Languages of Class, Studies in English Working Class History 1832–1982* (Cambridge: Cambridge University Press, 1983), pp. 137–40, discusses the relevance of Shelley's bullionism to the Chartists.
32 *Economic Essays*, p. 45.
33 For Keats's use of 'speculative' and 'speculation', see *Letters*, vol. I, pp. 175, 184–5, 223–4, 243, 277, 387; vol. II, pp. 80–1, 115. His aesthetic 'speculation' echoes the vocabulary which Burke, in *Reflections on the Revolution in France* . . . (1790), introduced by A. J. Grieve (London: Dent, 1910, 1967), famously attributed to an ungrounded dissenting imagination opposed to 'our nature . . . [and] the great conservatories and magazines of our rights and privileges' (pp. 32–3); but Keats is able culturally to accredit it because it lies, paradoxically, at the heart of that establishment's economic self-perpetuation. Burke had consistently inveighed against 'paper circulation, not founded on any real money ', and constantly punned on the theoretical and financial senses of 'speculation' in his attack on a revolutionary France 'founded . . . upon gaming', in which moral and political 'speculation [are] as extensive as life' (pp. 187–9). His diatribes against the 'fictitious wealth' of paper money are compromised both by his own use of all the resources of fiction to make his case, as Paine and others pointed out, and by the unspoken complicity between economic systems in France and England which were increasingly founded on sheer confidence. Keats's aesthetic then figures the departure from Burkean principle which made practicable Burkean constitutionalism.
34 David Simpson, *Wordsworth and the Figurings of the Real* (London: Macmillan, 1982), p. 159; Kurt Heinzelman, *The Economics of the Imagination* (Amhurst, Mass.: University of Massachusetts Press, 1980), p. 133.
35 [John Wilson Croker], *The Life, Adventures, & Serious Remonstrances of a Scottish Guinea Note, Containing a Defence of the Scottish System of Banking, and a Reply to the Late Letters of E. Bradwardine Waverly* (Edinburgh, 1826).
36 Karl Niebyl, *Studies in the Classical Theories of Money* (New York: Columbia University Press, 1946), p. 164; Levinson, *Keats's Life of Allegory*, pp. 288–9 and ch. 6, passim.
37 Marc Shell, *Money, Language, and Thought: Literary and Philosophical Economies from the Medieval to the Modern Era* (Berkeley, Los Angeles, London: University of California Press, 1982), p. 14. Levinson, reading the character Lamia as 'the money form', invokes support from the way in which G. Simmel's 'understanding of the renunciation inherent in the money form leads him to associate money with art', and argues that 'Simmel's definition of art is also a definition of the art we associate with the Romantic period': ibid., pp. 295–6.

Index

Abrams, M. H.   71, 82
absolutism   28
Adorno, Theodor   1, 11, 16n4, 61n30, 124, 126, 141n21
Aeschylus: *Agamemnon*   90, 91–2; *Eumenides*   90, 91, 92, 97; *Oresteia*   10, 89–94, 97–8, 105–6; *Prometheus Bound*   94; *Prometheus Unbound*   94
aesthetic: contradictions of the idealist   114–15, 118–20; economics of the   128–32
aesthetic scholarship   42, 61n31
aisthesis   122, 126
alienation   23, 81–2, 87–8
Althusser, Louis   7, 24, 51, 57n9, 60n28, n29, 61n32
American Romanticist orthodoxy, 81–2
Amiens, Peace of (1802)   39
anachronism, tautology in   12
ancien régime   25
'Ancients', the   98
Anglo-Saxon   67
Arab poetry   76–7
Arabian Nights   76–7
archives   11
Arendt, Hannah   138n3
Argos   91–3
Ariosto   73
Aristotle   105
Arnold, Matthew   11, 116
art, as agent of change   95–6, 99
articulateness, poetry as   136
Athens   89–92

Augustine, Saint   70
Austen, Jane   65

Bailey, Benjamin   116
Bakhtin   14, 97
ballads   67, 73
Bank of England   128–30: Restriction Act (1797)   129–30
barbarism, relation to culture   11, 86, 103
Barrell, John   4, 55n3, 59n21
Baudelaire, Charles Pierre   62n33, 104
Bayley, John   114
'beauties' rhetoric in Keats   115–16, 118–19
Benjamin, Walter   11, 36, 51, 86, 88, 103: 'The Task of the Translator' 52–5; 'Theses on the Philosophy of History'   86
Bennett, Tony   21
Bennington, Geoff   139n5
Berkeley, George   130: *Querist*   129
Bernstein, Michael, *The Tale of the Tribe*   107n25
Bewell, Alan   55n3
Bible   70, 76, 78, 105
Blackwell   66
Blackwood, William   118
Blackwood's   118
Blake, William   10, 15, 68, 71, 82, 95–101, 131: *Milton*   10, 99–100; *The Marriage of Heaven and Hell*   97
Bloom, Harold   71

Bourdieu, Pierre 138n3
bourgeois culture, Keats in relation to 109–13, 119–20, 126–7
British Critic 120
Bromwich, David 55n3
Brontës, the 65
Burke, Edmund 8, 78, 142n33
Burns, Robert 68
Butler, Marilyn 2, 3–4, 10–11, 55n3, 64–84: *Romantics, Rebels and Reactionaries* 3
Byron, George Gordon, Lord 3, 5, 6, 33, 68, 80–1, 82, 85, 114, 115–16: *Cain* 81; *Childe Harold's Pilgrimage* 101, 102; *Don Juan* 101, 102; 'Epistle to Augusta' 103; *The Giaour* 74, 81

California 71
Campbell, Thomas 129: *Pleasures of Hope* 83
Cannadine, David 64
canonical literature 11, 64–72: case against 69–71; impact on perception 68–9; new proposals 71–2; Victorian 67–9, 70
capital 127–32
capitalism 55n1, 98: transitions in 8
Carlyle, Thomas 71, 119
Cartesian idealism 25–31
causality, structural (Althusser) 7, 57n9, 61n32
Celtic culture 67
Chandler, Jim 55n3
change 24, 29, 33–4, 45, 77–8, 106: art as agent of 95–6; social 82–3
Chatterton, Thomas 73, 114, 121
Chaucer, Geoffrey 67, 114
Christensen, Jerome 8, 55n3
civilization, and barbarism 86, 103
Clark, J. C. D., *English Society: 1688–1832* 24
class conflict 32
Clough, Arthur Hugh 116
Coleridge, Samuel Taylor 3, 5, 8, 29, 33, 60n28, 68, 71, 73, 102, 118, 129: *Address to a Young Ass* 77; *Ancient Mariner* 77–9; *Biographia Literaria* 118; *Kubla Khan* 79; 'Monody' 121
Columbia University 71

comic modernist solution 62n35
commodity form 2, 21
consciousness: as absolute negativity 26, 43; alienated individual 81–2; in historicism 58n18; mode of and form of material production 44, 47; *see also* self-consciousness
constitution, retrospective 13
contemplation 2, 34, 50
contestation 3
contradiction 32–3, 46–9, 50, 53, 118–20: determinate 40, 59n21
Cornell University 66, 71
counter-transference 14
creed 35, 38, 60n23
crisis mentality 8
Critical Heritage 140n11
criticism: effect of canonical literature on 70–1, 116–17; framework for new historicist 22–3: must be abstract 9, 37, 53–4; must change 9, 40, 54; must give pleasure 9, 12, 54; politics in 19, 56n5; reflected 10; renunciation of 42; Romanticist 8–15; third world of 85–107
Croker, John Wilson 114, 117, 120, 123, 131–2
cross-referencing mode of analysis 56–7n5
culture: and politics 138n3; popular 29; relation to barbarism 11, 86, 103; relationship between state and 66–72
Cumberland, George 98

Dante Alighieri 114
de Man, Paul 133
deconstruction 10, 33, 39, 59n21, 66, 112
Defoe, Daniel, *The Chimera* 129
Delhi University, *Subaltern Studies* 66
democracy 93
Derrida, Jacques 138n3
Descartes, René 28–9, 57n15, 58n17; *see also* Cartesian idealism
detouring concept 9, 54
devaluation (Eliot) 19
dialectic: as immanent critique 4–5, 18, 20–1; Marxist historical 32–3;

Index

master–slave 58n18; of old historicism 2, 30
dialogism (Bakhtin) 14
difference 32–3, 52, 106: structural 40, 59n21
difference principle *see* Cartesian idealism
Dilthey, Wilhelm 24, 30–1
displacement 11–12
domination 86–7
doubling 113
dualism 6–9, 62–3n35

Eagleton, Terry 139n5
Edinburgh Review 130
education, in literature 65–72
Eliot, George (Mary Ann Evans) 65
Eliot, Thomas Stearns 19, 62n35
Elizabethan lyric and drama 67
Emerson, Ralph Waldo 71
empathy 2, 29, 34, 50
empiricism 22
English literature 64–72: teaching of 69–70
Enlightenment historiography 24–31
Enlightenment materialism 25–31, 35
Enlightenment progress poem 9
Ephialtes 89, 90, 92
error, and truth of poetry 14–15
essentialism 21, 66
eternity 100–1
evaluation 70–1
Evangelical Movement, nineteenth-century 98

Fanon, Frantz 11, 88, 94: 'Concerning Violence' 85–6, 87; 'On National Culture' 86–7
fascism 62n35, 104
Fichte, Johann Gottlieb 118
Fish, Stanley 21
folk culture 76
formalism 20, 21
Formtrieb–Stofftrieb dualism 35, 41, 60n28
Foucault, Michel 97, 126
freedom 44, 58n15
Freud, Sigmund 12–14, 63n35, 71
Frye, Northrop 71

fulfilment, idea 115, 117, 118, 124: critique in Keats 120–1
future 18–63, 87, 97, 101
'futurity' (Shelley) 93–4

Gaelic poetry 76
Genesis 94
Ghandi, Rajiv 65
Gifford, William 111
Gilchrist, Alexander 98
Gillray, James, *The Anti-Jacobin* 84n7
Goldstein, Laurence 55n3
Gothic tales 67
Gray, Thomas 67, 76
Greeks 35–8, 41–2, 60n29, 61n31
Greenblatt, Stephen 19

Haggard, Rider: *King Solomon's Mines* 74; *She* 74
Hamilton, Paul 11, 55n3, 108–42
Hamilton, Sir William 118, 140n12
Hart, Francis R. 140n12
Hartman, Geoffrey 71
Harvester 66
Haydon, Benjamin Robert 117
Hazlitt, William 111, 116–17
Hegel, Georg Wilhelm Friedrich 2, 4, 6, 25, 29, 32, 71, 100, 102, 108, 114, 126
Heinzelman, Kurt 55n3, 131
Herbert, George 115
Herodotus 105
heroic ideal 82
Hinduism 80–1
historian, ideal 13
historicism: comparison and relations of new with old 20–2, 24–34, 52; 'dilemma' of 30, 31–3; new (Levinson) 18–63; nineteenth-century 28–31; relations of new and old with Romanticism 1–6, 25–34; use of term 18, 55n4
history: British 64; meaning of 105
Holbach, Paul Heinrich Dietrich 29
Homer 92
Horkheimer, Max 61n30
humanism 113
humanities 65–6
humanization 27, 29
Hume, David 129, 130, 141n28

Hunt, Leigh   114, 115–16
Hutcheson, Frances   130

idealism   2, 10
ideation, act of   9
ideology   14, 46–9, 56n5, 60–1n29, 61n30: inadequacy of new historicist concept   49–51; problematizing of the work's own   5–6; *see also* Romantic ideology
Imaginary (Lacan)   12
imagination: imperial   95, 103; non-colonialist   85–107
immortalist illusion   100–1
imperialism   86–8, 93, 100, 104
India   65, 66, 81
interventions   7–8
irony   51–3, 62n33: Romantic, reflexivity of   135–6
islanding of works of culture   88–9

Jameson, Fredric   10, 54, 60n25
Jeffrey, Francis   72, 73, 77, 79
Joan of Arc   81
Johnson, Samuel   11
Johnston, Kenneth   55n3
Jones, John   122
Jones, William   76
Jonson, Ben   47
Joseph, Bertram   139n9
Joyce, James   62n35
judgement, by translation   48, 50, 52–5

Kant, Immanuel   71, 102, 108, 126, 138n3
Kantian aesthetic   2, 6, 8, 15, 95, 100–1, 105, 110, 113, 118, 119–20, 122
Kean, Edmund   115, 139n9
Keats, John   11, 12, 68, 70, 72, 82: and critique   108–42; *Endymion*   114, 115–17, 119–25, 131; *Eve of St Agnes*   114, 125; *Hyperion*   133–6; *Lamia*   74; 'Lines on the Mermaid Tavern'   137; 'Ode on a Grecian Urn'   112–13; 'Ode to Psyche'   122, 135; *The Fall of Hyperion*   2, 135–7
Kierkegaard, Søren   32

Kimon   89, 90
kitsch   126–7, 133, 138n3, 141n21
knowledge   2, 14, 50, 55n1, 58n15
Korea   65

LaCapra, Dominick   8, 12–14
Lacan, Jacques   12
Lacoue-Labarthes, Philippe   7–8
Landor, Walter Savage, *Gebir*   83
language: disorganized   14, 16n16; Romantic ideology in   17n16
Latin, future of   67
Law, John   128, 129, 130, 131
Levinson, Marjorie   1–17, 18–63, 118, 119, 129, 132, 142n37: *Keats's Life of Allegory – The Origins of a Style*   109–10
Linnell, John   98
literacy, mass   67
literalism   53–5, 133
literary canon *see* canonical literature
literary history: case for open   64–84; teaching of   66–72, 84
literary research, effect of canonical literature on   70
literature, in English   64–5: teaching of   65–72
Liu, Alan   55n3
Locke, John   65, 128
Lockhart, John Gibson   117, 118, 119, 121: *Peter's Letters to his Kinsfolk*   118
Lowth, Robert   76
Lukács, Georg   55n1
Lyotard, Jean-François   15, 127

Macdonald, George   74
McGann, Jerome   2, 6, 10–11, 14, 17n16, 55n3, 85–107, 112: *Social Values and Poetic Acts*   2; *The Romantic Ideology*   13
Macpherson, James   76
Marx, Karl   25, 31–4, 58n20
Marxian critical methods and values in new historicism   4, 20–2, 63n35
Marxist dialectical materialism   31–4, 47
materialism: Enlightenment   25–31, 38–9, 58n15; Marxist dialectically

historical 31–4; new 10, 110
matter 31: and mind 33–4, 58n18, n20
meaning 10, 58n15
meanings: choice of 19–20, 23–4; futurity of 93–4
Mellor, Anne 55n3
Methuen 66
Meyerhoff, Hans, *The Philosophy of History in Our Time* 24
middle class: critique of 35, 44; emergence of 27–30; *see also* bourgeois culture
Mill, John Stuart, *Examination* 118
Milton, John 41, 45, 65, 96, 114, 115: *Paradise Lost* 99
mind 28: and matter 33–4, 58n18, n20
mirror image 7, 12
Modernism 71, 105
modernization 94
Mohammedanism 77
'molarity' 57n5
Montagu, Lady Mary Wortley 65
Montrose, Louis 19
Moore, Tom 129: *Lalla Rookh* 80
Morris, Wesley, *Towards a New Historicism* 24
Murray, Les 69

Nancy, Jean-Luc 7–8
Napoleonic image 25–8
narrative principle, refusal of 22
National Curriculum, Department of Education and Science 69–70
nationalism 67, 69
Nature 30, 32–4, 47, 133
negation 25, 26, 59n21
negativity 43
neologisms, Wordsworth's 48
New England canon 71
New Jerusalem Church 97–8
Niebyl, Karl 132
Nietzsche, Friedrich Wilhelm 71, 97, 105
Norse poetry 67, 76

objectification, law of 16n4
objectivity 4, 7, 9, 88
objects (Descartes) 57n15

oppositions, standard binary (LaCapra) 13

paper money controversies 128–30
parataxis 122–5, 133
Patmore, Coventry 139n9
Peacock, Thomas Love: *Four Ages of Poetry* 129; *Paper Money Lyrics* 129
Pechter, Edward 1
Peloponnesian Wars 93
Pepys, Samuel 67
Pericles 89, 92, 95
'periplum' (Pound) 102
Petrarch 114
phenomenology 31, 128
philosophy 60n25, 105
Pindar 76
pleasure: criticism must give 9, 12, 54; Keatsian critique of 124–5
poet, as creation of the age 3
poet-critic, as self-made maker 62n33
poetry: historically overdetermined 105–6; redemption of the social order function 95–6
politicizing, active, of text 21–3, 46–7, 96–100
politics 7–9, 11, 19, 25, 43, 55n4, 56n5: culture and 109–12, 138n3; and social needs 83–4
Pope, Alexander 47
populism 74, 83
positivism 10, 20
post-modernism 15, 127
post-structuralism 10, 56n5, 65
Pound, Ezra 10, 62n35: *Cantos* 10, 45, 101–6; *Drafts and Fragments* 103
power 2, 4, 50, 66–72
pragmatism 21
precipitation 47, 49
Proctor, B. W. 139n9
production, mode of, and form of consciousness 44, 47, 48, 56n5
progress, human 77–9
progression–regression (Sartre) 49, 57n10, 59n21
prophecy 5, 13, 21, 82, 95
psychoanalytical model 12–14
pun, reflexive 112–13
Puritan Revolution 45

Quarterly 111, 116, 117, 118
quest: critique of spiritual 79; for Total Form 102–3

Rand, Richard 138n4
Ranke, Leopold von 24, 30–1
rationalism 4
reader, the 'distanced' 104–5
reading 64, 106, 114: self-ironizing 62n33
Real, the 26, 51, 54, 56n4, 60n28, 61n29
Reason 25, 28, 40
reception history 22, 97–8
redundancy of Romantic aesthetic, Keats's critique of 115, 133–6
reflection 2, 10, 49
refusal 3, 22, 49, 88
reification 13, 22, 49
relation, modes of, as object of new historicist criticism 10–15, 20–3
relativism 20, 21, 30
religion 60n25
repetition 13–14
representation 24, 26, 54, 56n5
resistance to symbolization 3, 15, 32, 51, 54; *see also* refusal
Revolution 25–31, 35, 38, 45, 81, 83
Revolutionary drama 30
Ricardo, David 141n22: Ingot Plan 129–30; *The High Price of Bullion* 130–1
Richmond, George 98
Ricks, Christopher 125
Robinson, Crabb 139n9
Roman Catholicism 77
Romantic, use of category 2
Romantic aesthetic, Keats's immanent critique of the 110, 132–7
Romantic ideology 18, 22, 95, 99
Romantic studies, new historicism in 18–63
'Romanticism, Politics and the New Historicism', UCLA Conference 2
Romanticism, relations with old and new historicism 25–34
Rose, Jacqueline 16n5
Rousseau, Jean Jacques 77: *On the Origins and Foundations of Inequality among Men* 76

rule-by-efficiency 4
Ruskin, John 65

Sahlins, Marshall, *Islands of History* 106n8
Sartre, Jean Paul 23, 49, 54, 57n9, n10, 61n29, 62n35
Saussure, Ferdinand de 126
Schiller, Johann Christoph Friedrich von 41, 60n28, 113, 118, 127
Schlegel, August Wilhelm von 21
Schlegel, Friedrich, *Vorlesungen über die Geschichte der alten und neue Literatur* 118
Scott, John 116
Scott, Sir Walter 68, 129
Scottish literature 67
self, anxieties of Romantic 43–4
self-consciousness 25–6, 29, 43, 55n1
self-criticism, poetic, ironies of 6, 111, 116–37
sensuousness, Keats's 113, 119–20, 122, 126, 132
Shaffer, Elinor 62n33
Shakespeare, William 65, 70, 117
Shell, Marc 132
Shelley, Mary: *Frankenstein* 74; *Posthumous Works* 80
Shelley, Mary: *Frankenstein* 74; *Posthumous Works* 80
Shelley, Percy Bysshe 3, 6, 7, 15, 16n16, 61n31, 68, 71, 76, 79–81, 82, 93, 95, 96, 108, 116: *Alastor* 80; 'Cenci, The' 2; *Prometheus Unbound* 3, 94; *Queen Mab* 80, 81, 130; *The Mask of Anarchy* 130; *The Revolt of Islam* 80; *The Witch of Atlas* 79
'Shining, The' 54.
shock 54
Sidney, Sir Phillip 115
Simmel, Georg 126, 142n37
Simpson, David 55n3, 131
Siskin, Cliff 55n3
Smith, Adam 68, 130
Smith, Olivia 55n3
'social text' 56n4
Southey, Robert 3, 5, 72–84, 129: *Curse of Kehama* 76, 79, 80–1, 82; *Thalaba* 3, 73–80, 82–3

Sparta 89–90, 92
Spenser, Edmund 73, 114
Spieltrieb 41
Spinoza, Baruch 6
Spivak, Gayatri, *In Other Worlds* 66
state, relationship between culture and 66–72
Steuart, Sir James 129
Stevens, Wallace 11, 45, 62n35, 71: 'Notes Toward a Supreme Fiction' 9
Stoker, Bram, *Dracula* 74
Studies in Romanticism 109
style 56n5
subjectivity 7, 9, 20, 24, 30–1
subjects (Descartes) 57n15
Swift, Jonathan 47
systems analysis 20

Tasso, Torquato 73
Tatham, Frederick 98
tautology 12, 114–15, 118, 133, 134–5
Taylor, Jeremy 78
temporality 22, 50: complex repetitive 8, 13
Tennyson, Alfred Lord 67
text: active politicizing of 21–3; 'social' 56n4
Thatcher, Margaret 4, 11, 65
theology, 'displaced' 82
Third Imagination 86–8
Third World 66
Thucydides 105
Times Literary Supplement 64
Tolkien, J. R. R. 74
Total Form, idea of 102–3
totalization (Sartre) 23, 54, 57n9, 59n21, 88
transference 8, 12–14

translation, judgement by 49, 50, 52–5
transparency 15, 50
truth of poetry 14–15
Tyler, Wat 81

USA 64–5, 71
utopian dreams 89–94

Veblen, Thorstein 141n22
Verso 66
Vico, Giovanni Battista 29, 33
violence 11–12, 86–7

Warhol, Andy 127
Wellek, René 140n12
Welsh literature 67, 76
Whigham, Frank 19
White, Hayden 24
Whitman, Walt 71
wit 11–12
Wohlfarth, Irving 1
Wolfson, Susan 62n33, 109
women, and literature 68–9
Woodring, Carl 2
Wordsworth, William 3, 5, 12, 14, 25, 34, 65, 68, 70, 71, 72, 80, 82, 96, 114, 118, 121, 123, 124, 129, 131, 133: *Intimations of Immortality* 39–40; *Lyrical Ballads* 73; 'Nuns fret not' 36; 'Ode to Duty' 46; 'The Borderers' 38; 'The Idiot Boy' 118; *The Prelude* 2, 79, 81, 82; 'The world is too much with us' 35–49

Yale 66, 71: resistance to 19, 23, 55n4
Yeats, William Butler, 'Leda and the Swan' 55